TABLE OF CONTENTS

DEDICATION

This book is dedicated to my kids, Kierra and Logan. You mean more to me than you will ever know, and I am deeply grateful to God for blessing me with the two of you. And although your K-12 school years are over, I would still remind you to:
Work hard.
Do your best.
Have fun.
Be kind. And —
I love you.

ACKNOWLEDGMENTS

Every book (well, many books anyway) acknowledges family members who have supported the author on her journey – a spouse, children and sometimes parents or siblings. That's true for me as well. I am grateful for the love and support (and patience) of my immediate and extended family. But I would be remiss if I didn't also acknowledge the teachers who inspired and taught me throughout my entire life. I can still name every homeroom teacher I had from Kindergarten through 8th grade (as well as most of the other grade-level teachers), and my "subject matter teachers" in high school. Although all contributed to who I am today, there are a few who really stand out, for very specific reasons.

- *Marilyn John* – Mrs. John was my 3rd grade teacher, and encouraged me to be a writer in a unique way – *years* after I left her classroom as a student. Just one teacher who ignited the love of writing in me all those years ago has made this book possible. If you are a teacher, never underestimate the impact you may have on a student.
- *Sue Nystrom and Mary Bramer* – 6th grade team teachers who went above and beyond to support me the year my dad died. Their extravagant compassion, care, and flexibility got me through that terrible year.

- *Jodell White* – my high school choir director who taught me excellence, discipline, perseverance, and hard work, not only in music, but in all things. Music remains a life-giving joy to me all these years later, and the life skills and disciplines she taught remain a cornerstone of who I am and who I strive to be.
- *Alice Marnin* – Alice didn't hold the title of teacher, but her unconditional love and support taught me much about how to live in this world, even when bad things happened. Compassion and kindness, encouragement, and devotion to God were and are the hallmarks of her life, and I am eternally grateful to know her.

And, of course, Curt Patterson, the mentor to end all mentors. Your support through some difficult times in my life has meant the world to me. Your perspective, honesty, and a refusal to allow me to get stuck in those hard times was of immeasurable value to me, and I thank you for it. May God continue to bless you.

Finally, I want to thank my editor, Deb Engle. Your support, encouragement, and honest assessment of my work have made this a wonderful, fulfilling experience. Your insight and prompt turn-around times kept this project moving quickly, helping me to fulfill a lifelong dream. Thank you.

INTRODUCTION

I did not set out to write a book about letting go. The stories in this book started out as journal entries—a way to try to make sense of the struggles I was having in my life, the ones that seemed to come in waves, one right after, or sometimes on top of one another. It wasn't until I had written several entries that I was able to see the common theme of letting go (or, to be more precise, the *refusal* to let go). But even then, there was no intention to share the stories in a book. These experiences were too personal, too raw. I felt exposed just *writing* about them, let alone *sharing* them.

But then I remembered an experience I had while serving on the Board of Deacons at my church. In addition to our Sunday duties, we had a board meeting once a month. At the beginning of each of those meetings, one or two of us would do a "devotional." These weren't the traditional read-from-a-book and then read-a-prayer kinds of devotionals. Instead, we were to answer three questions. The questions changed from year to year, but they were always (if you let them be) deeply personal. The year I did my devotional, the questions had to do with who we thought God was, both as a child and then as an adult.

I spoke about what I called a "nasty run-in with God" at the age of 12. The story is included in this book, so I won't spoil the details here. But it was a *deeply* personal story, and I confess I struggled to keep the tears at bay. I could hear others "sniffing," and when I stopped, it was very, very still. It had made an impact. David Ruhe, senior pastor at the time, wove much of what I said into his closing prayer. Many people approached me after the meeting to tell me how much my story had touched them.

To paraphrase David (who freely admits that the quote wasn't his originally), our most personal experiences are also the most universal. It occurred to me that sharing these stories was a way to connect with people in a way that a typical "business book" or even self-help book would not. The very intimacy of the stories made them compelling.

There were some stories, however, that I ultimately decided were *too* personal to share. These were primarily relationship stories, and while I would have been willing to share them, I wasn't sure the "other party" would be as willing to see him or herself in print, especially given that it was *my* side of the story, with no chance for them to respond. Anne Lamott once famously (at least famously to writers) wrote, "You own everything that happened to you. Tell your stories. If people wanted you to write warmly about them, they should have behaved better." While I find great humor (and a certain amount of truth) in this quote, I'm not quite willing to *follow* it in all cases yet.

Writing has always been a way for me to process my thoughts, especially given my introverted nature. Some people are worried about "confessing" things in writing, out of fear that they might fall into the wrong hands. But here's what I discovered: you can always hit delete or otherwise get rid of the journals.

At one point in my life, I had a number of journals. I lugged those journals around from move to move, never considering that I was also taking the negativity that they contained as well. After one particularly anguishing move, I found myself sitting on the floor, cross-legged, reading the journals as I unpacked them. With every page, I felt worse and worse. It was like willingly jumping into a dark pool, with no idea which way was up. The journals not only revealed how deeply unhappy I was, but also how often I was "failing." I was *so*—stuck. And in reading my journals, I was "reminding" myself of all the times I had failed.

Suddenly, in the middle of all that swirling darkness, a bright light burst through with a simple command. *"Get rid of them!"* Without questioning this, I immediately jumped up and headed to the dumpster with an armful of journals. I pitched them in, realizing that all the pain they represented was now where it belonged—in the trash. Walking back, I had a strange sensation of exhilarated peace. There was no sense of regret or panic ("Oh, no! What have I *done?*"). It felt like a new beginning, with none of the baggage of past mistakes.

Symbolic? Sure. Effective? Yes.

Of course, when you tell people you have thrown away handwritten journals, some are horrified. And I get it. It's a part of who you are, and a part of your history—and now it's lost forever. But this was not a legacy I wanted to leave behind for others to find and read. One woman was brave enough to ask me if I regretted throwing them away. I emphatically said no. I explained that once I let go of the journals, I felt much lighter. Not only was I letting go of the physical journals and freeing up the space they were occupying on my shelves, but I was also freeing myself of the negativity and disappointment that were tied to them. I didn't need to be reminded of the things that had gone wrong. Those things *were* best lost forever.

So writing the stories that are in this book was a process for me to honestly work through my struggles, to look for patterns and solutions while knowing that I could always destroy the "evidence" later.

At the same time I was continuing this written journey, I committed to writing a book and getting it published. I had talked about doing that for a number of years but had never actually *done* it. I was trying to do too many other things at the same time, desperately jumping from one thing to another to try and find the "right" thing. In early January, exhausted by all this flailing about, I sat quietly in prayer and wearily said, "Ok, God. I need some help here. I know I'm supposed to make a certain number of 'sales' calls here, but I honestly don't know whom to call. Will you just give me those names so I can do it?"

I did not get an answer. Instead, I got a question. "*What if you gave yourself permission to simply* write *for the next 12 weeks?*"

I literally gasped out loud. Could I *do* that? My mentor would *never* stand for me pulling out of prospecting to write! I got no response to my arguments. I finally quieted down enough to actually consider the question. What if I *did* focus on my writing for 12 weeks? And then a great sense of relief swept through me—it would be *wonderful beyond belief* if I could "just" write!

So I did.

When I sent my editor my proposed book—a safe, but boring one—I, to paraphrase a statement I once made to my son, "received a 'grade' commensurate to the amount of effort I put into it." And by effort, I mean, my willingness to boldly tell *my* story, rather than share vanilla information that lots of other business writers have shared. I questioned whether I should let go of my dream to be a writer—for about two seconds. No, that definitely was not the right answer.

For the next four days, I thought about it. I prayed about it. And the response I received was, "*You sent her the wrong book.*"

And though I tried to resist that thought, I was, as my mentor says, *convicted* by the truth of the statement.

And terrified. Definitely terrified.

Given that my recent pleadings with God have been something along the lines of, "Just tell me what to do and I will do it," I really was in no position to now say, "Well, except for that. I won't do *that.*" So, I took a deep breath and, with great trepidation, sent a few sample chapters.

Did I mention I was terrified?

And, of course, she *loved* that book.

As I sat at my computer, reading her remarks, I found myself looking heavenward, saying, "Really? *This* is the book you want me to publish?" I sighed, because I knew that the answer to that question, no matter how much I resisted, was yes.

A few months before, during my quiet prayer time, the message "you can help a lot of people" had been clearly imprinted on my heart. The stark differences in my editor's response to the two books I had submitted made clear that writing the "safe" book would not have nearly the impact or potential to help people as would the "dangerous" book.

The safe book might help people do some of the tactical things better, but it would never transform someone's life. The dangerous book, on the other hand, did have that potential. It would help people know they were not alone, that it was okay—in fact, imperative—to let some beliefs, things, and even people—go.

But did I *really* have to be *this* transparent? Could I get away with sharing a little less information? I wrestled mightily with this. One day I was determined to move forward. The next I was offering up the reasons excuses as to why it wouldn't work. But God kept getting ahead of me, providing the answer to the obstacle before it appeared.

I asked, quite reasonably, where the money was going to come from for this little "project." And I received a credit card with zero interest that would cover it. My husband's company was going through bankruptcy, and although his job was safe, his salary wasn't. I suggested to God, again quite reasonably, that perhaps I shouldn't spend the money on the book right now. God sent me a coaching client and some church accompanying work. Publishing the book would force me to have a particularly difficult conversation that I had been putting off for years. *Years.* That conversation turned out to be neither as scary nor as problematic as I feared. And now I had cleared out another obstacle to getting the book done.

But at the time, I didn't know how any of that was going to work out. I didn't have the credit card, the work or the conversation. I was (as I think I've mentioned once or twice) terrified, and those negative voices took full advantage of that terror. I had written blog posts boldly proclaiming that instead of creating New Year's Resolutions, I had chosen to use a theme to guide my decisions. In 2015, I had the sheer audacity to choose *Be Strong and Courageous* as my theme. But *seriously*—was publishing this book courageous? Or just plain stupid? The fraud factor kicked into high gear—would anyone even *like* me if they knew who I *really* was—mistakes, flaws and all?

Clearly, the first thing I would have to let go of was my attachment to what other people thought of me, as well as my own punishing self-talk. Could I really be as brave as the message in Little Big Town's song "Boondocks?"

"You can take it or leave it. This is me. This is who I am."

I began to truly consider what that might mean. It might reveal pretty clearly who my real friends were. It would definitely be easier to no longer avoid questions about why we moved, or how come I was no longer speaking to a certain long-time friend. There wouldn't be anything left to hide. And *that* might be a great relief. Hmmmm…maybe I *could* write this book.

And yet.

I still felt a little bit like Debra Messing's character, Kat, in the movie *The Wedding Date.* Kat lives in New York, having escaped her dysfunctionally normal family in England. But now her sister is getting married, and she's going back home for an event that does not always bring out the best in families.

She and her sister have always been competitive, and with her sister getting married, and Kat's ex-fiancé as the best man, the pressure is on Kat to bring a fabulous date. There's only one problem—she's not seeing anyone—fabulous or otherwise. So she does the "logical" thing—she *hires* Mr. Fabulous.

When the courier comes to pick up her date's plane ticket, Kat offers the envelope but can't seem to release her grip. The courier frowns and states the obvious: "You're going to have to let go." And in one of the most understated yet profound lines of the movie, she says, "You're going to have to help me."

I often feel that way. I know there are things I need to let go of, yet I'm so afraid of what might happen if I do, that I can't seem to release my death grip on them. I clearly need to let go, but I'm going to need some help.

The problem is, when *fate* "helps" me let go, it's often brutal, mainly because I've held on way too long. Even when this was pointed out to me during a quiet prayer time at St. Augustine's Prayer Chapel, I still struggled. "*Surely I don't have to let go of THIS,*" I would protest. "*You want me to let go of him? Everyone else says I'm not supposed to let go of him!*"

Sometimes I have to let go of things because of bad decisions I've made. Sometimes I have to let go because I've simply outgrown someone. Sometimes I don't have to let go of a particular person so much as the *belief* I have about that person or his or her role in my life.

Although I am not a *physical* hoarder, I am definitely an *emotional* hoarder. Letting go, or surrendering, is not something that's natural for me—or most everyone else, frankly. It requires considerable courage and trust. It requires faith that all things *can* work together for good. It demands that we release our expectations of what *should* happen and how people will behave toward us, as well as our insistence that our life follow a rigid, planned path.

But here's the ironic thing. When I actually do let go, one of two things usually happens. Either it comes right back to me, or it makes room for something much better to come into my life. It's a reminder to not get too attached to our preconceived ideas or expected outcomes—or even people or things. The lesson is *not* that we aren't *allowed* to have those ideas, people or things, just that we shouldn't try to *force* them into our lives.

My grandmother taught me this very thing. When you try to force things, they're likely to break. Although she was talking about physical things, I've found it to be just as true in relationships and desires—whether professional or personal. The times when I have tried to force things to happen in a certain way (e.g., law school— that one was a doozy) are the times that have had the greatest negative repercussions—the greatest "brokenness" and failure.

In the movie, when Kat lets go of the tickets so they can be delivered to Mr. Fabulous, she goes on the ride of her life, but ultimately, she wins. She wins the love of a man who truly cherishes her just as she is. But it never would have happened if she had not been brave and let go of the tickets (and the ex-fiancé, but that's another story).

The question in our lives is not, "*Are* there things I need to let go of?" because there are—I'm sure of it. The real question is, are we courageous enough to let go of those beliefs, things and people?

Take a deep breath. Let go.

NOTE ABOUT CHARACTERS

All of the stories in this book are true—to the best of my recollection and perception, anyway. They share lessons I have learned about letting go, sometimes joyfully, but often painfully. Life, of course, does not occur in a vacuum with no supporting characters. Some of the people in this book are named, because either they're people like my kids (whose identity is obvious to anyone who knows me, and easy to find out for anyone who doesn't), or people I want to acknowledge for their significant contributions to my life and growth (like my mentor). Credit where credit is due, so to speak.

But others, whose lessons have been equally valuable, may not appreciate my sharing the *way* these lessons were taught or their involvement in the lesson. It is *not* my intention to embarrass or shame anyone. And just because *I* have decided to be totally transparent in the telling of my story does not mean that *they* want to find themselves or their stories in my book in an equally transparent way.

In those cases, I have changed names and identifying factors. If you find a character in this book that you suspect might be you, however, please understand that *even if you are right* (which you might not be), I am deeply grateful for the lesson (even if I might not have been so at the time!) and your role in imparting said lesson. I have forgiven everyone (even the boss from Hades referenced in one story), and hope that you have forgiven me my shortcomings and failures.

I wish only abundant blessings for all of you—even if I have "let you go."

CHAPTER 1

THE HOUSE

I often visit St. Augustine's prayer chapel, which initially was a little weird for this born-and-raised Methodist girl. Several years ago, when I was still practicing law, a colleague of mine told me about it, saying that it was open 24/7, solely for prayer. The first time I worked up my courage to go, I slunk in, sliding into the back pew as though someone might "catch" me. It reminded me of a story my husband's aunt used to tell. Apparently her Presbyterian mother (Randy's grandmother) was having a bad Sunday. As she regaled everyone with the details, she concluded by saying, "And to top it all off, there was a *Methodist* in the back row!" Well here I was—the Methodist in the back row.

I wasn't sure how to "act" in a Catholic prayer chapel, so I surreptitiously watched others. Some knelt, some had rosary beads, and some simply sat quietly. I tried kneeling, but the discomfort in my knees was too distracting. I wouldn't know what to do with rosary beads if I had them, so I opted to simply sit in stillness. People came in, knelt, crossed themselves, and then rose and went to their seat. I began feeling a bit self-conscious—would they figure out I was an infiltrator—a non-Catholic—and ask me to leave? Well, no.

It seems rather ridiculous now to think they might, but at the time, it seemed a real possibility—I was so obviously *not* Catholic.

After getting over the anxiety, I found I really liked it there. It's a place of such complete quiet—an ideal place to go when I just need to think, uninterrupted. People do not talk to each other, there is no music playing in the background, and only one time have I ever heard a cell phone ring (and the woman to whom the phone belonged scurried out so quickly, you would have thought that was the eighth deadly sin!). While I don't claim to "hear" voices, the absolute quiet helps me to focus and allows the answers to simply come to me without all the "static" and distractions of other locations.

I always take a journal and a pen because I want to capture anything God cares to share with me in that sacred space. I often have something specific I want to "visit" with Him about, but sometimes, things spring up unbidden and seemingly without any connection to what I am thinking about.

There's really no rhyme or reason as to when these things surface; there's nothing memorable about the day or the weather or the people there. My routine is always to go in and sit down, take a few deep breaths, and get myself settled. I read the words inscribed at the front—"They shall make for me a sanctuary, that I might dwell in their midst"—and then begin looking at the people who are there. I don't know them, but for some reason, I always feel compelled to pray for them. Do I think they need healing or comfort? Guidance? I have no way of knowing, of course, but I do like the ritual of praying for them first before bringing my own concerns to God.

On one of these average, routine days of prayer, a decidedly *un-average* thought presented itself for consideration: "*You hang on to things too long, which causes significantly more pain when they finally 'leave.'*" I sat, suddenly very still. Wow. Where did *that* come from?

Hanging on to things, of course, is classic scarcity thinking. You believe that you might *never* again have the thing you are hanging on to (or the "I might need this someday" philosophy of a hoarder), so you are loath to let it go. But hanging on to things too long means there is no room for new, better things to come into your life. As Dr. Henry Cloud, author of *Necessary Endings* says, "[G]ood cannot begin until bad ends."

Here's how this played out in my life a few years back. Be fore-warned—this is a difficult story for me to tell. Because of the shame associated with it, I will probably do too much explaining. But—I'm still going to explain.

In 2008, my husband had quintuple bypass surgery. Although we had insurance, it's still not a cheap procedure, especially when you spend nine days in the hospital (seven of those nine in cardiac intensive care). Shortly after that, I decided to start my own consulting business. It started off well, but then the financial collapse of 2008 happened. The fear and economic uncertainty dried up consulting opportunities almost overnight. I decided the "smartest" thing to do was to head back to the field of law and get a "job." Unfortunately, because of the recession and the fact that so many people were suddenly out of work, every time I applied for a position, 100 of my closest attorney friends were also applying for the same position. Needless to say, I was unable to find work.

I wondered if perhaps law *wasn't* where I should be looking. It certainly wasn't what I longed to do. I decided that while I would still look for a job in the legal field, I would also pursue a more creative line of work. At one point, I applied for a staff writing position at a large publishing company in town. I knew it was an entry level writing position, but I was willing to start at the bottom and work my way up. In an odd twist, I was told I was both under- *and* over-qualified for the position. I was over-qualified because I had a law degree, and this was an entry-level job. I was under-qualified because my degree wasn't in Journalism or English. Never mind that writing was an integral part of a successful law practice—I wasn't "qualified."

And although people say that they would take whatever job they could get if they were in that situation, I am here to tell you that when you have a law degree, retail establishments are not anxious to hire you. They assume you will quit as soon as something better comes along. And to be fair, they are probably right. You can't leave the law degree off the application, though, because then you have "lied."

Doors were slamming—decisively—everywhere I knocked.

In 2009, we got behind on our mortgage payments. I had taken over the bill-paying duties after Randy had his heart surgery because I was trying to protect him from stress. But I was quickly getting backed into a corner. I could pay the mortgage and a few other bills, or I could pay the other bills and not the mortgage. Keeping the lights on and the water running seemed a more immediate need. This decision to address the most immediate, pressing need at the expense of the big picture is called "tunneling," but at the time, I just knew that if I didn't pay the water bill, we weren't going to have any water in a few days. It plays on a weird sense of desperate optimism—*surely* I would get a job soon, and I could get caught up on the mortgage.

Instead, the bank filed a foreclosure action.

I didn't want to call any attorneys I knew, largely because of the shame factor. And, of course, the fact that there was no money in the budget for legal fees. I tried Legal Aid, but upon learning that I was an attorney, the lawyer I spoke with made it clear that I should be able to help myself and leave their meager resources to those who truly needed their assistance.

But I knew nothing about that area of law. I had practiced in family and employment law. Asking me to represent someone in a foreclosure action would be like asking a pediatrician to perform arthroscopic surgery. And *if* I had tried to represent clients in a foreclosure action (unless I had assistance from an attorney experienced in that area of the law), I would have potentially faced ethics charges because I would not have been qualified to represent them. But since I was just representing myself, Legal Aid decided I should do it myself.

Cast adrift, I did the best I could.

In April 2010, I reached an agreement with the bank to make forbearance payments for three months, beginning in May. Forbearance payments are a reduced mortgage payment and are designed to be temporary, to get you through an unexpected financial challenge.

The bank's own falsely encouraging documentation claimed that one of the ways to avoid foreclosure was to have a forbearance agreement, which would not only get money going toward the mortgage again, but also provide time for the bank and the homeowner to rework the mortgage agreement. I was told multiple times by various representatives that the new mortgage payment amount (based in part on a reduced interest rate) would be "about" the same as the forbearance payments. Great! It seemed there was a light at the end of the tunnel.

Despite the bank's repeated assurances, however, we did not have a new mortgage by the time of the court hearing. I argued to the court (the law degree *did* come in handy here) that we had a forbearance agreement with the bank, that we were in compliance with that agreement, and as such, they could not foreclose, pursuant to their own documentation. The judge agreed.

Dan Stevens, the attorney who was representing the bank, asked that rather than dismiss the action (since it had only been a few months), the court continue the hearing until October so that if we were not in compliance, they would not have to start all over again. The judge reasonably agreed and, in October, dismissed the case because we *were* still making payments. We were in compliance.

I stepped up my efforts to get the bank to redo the mortgage as they said they would. Time I could have been spent looking for work was instead spent pacing the living room, either on hold or arguing with my "designated representative." There were "hot mic" moments when representatives made rude remarks, thinking I couldn't hear them. Different representatives would give me different answers and even different advice about sending in payments. My frustration and stress level grew, and I confess that I was not a very nice person at times. I am at my worst when I am afraid. I would take deep breaths and start over, trying to be as patient as I could.

In response, the bank delayed, telling me they were "overwhelmed" and would get to it when they could. I continued to pay the forbearance amount, but in January (after making nine months of consistent payments) and again in February the bank rejected payments. I asked why they would reject payments (does that even make sense?), and they told me that I had neglected to provide a particular document, which to this day has never been identified.

I had provided *reams* of documents; it's hard to imagine what they *didn't* have. Stacks and file folders of documents, neatly organized by correspondence, legal documents, bank documents, employment documents and miscellaneous documents. Every month we had to provide our checking and savings account statements, increasing the size of that stack. We had to provide copies of Randy's pay stubs, tax returns and monthly expenses. We were drowning in documents, and yet there was still *one* that we had apparently not provided. It's possible that the document they sought didn't even exist, or that they already had it, buried somewhere in their own stack—both had happened before. But because the bank refused to identify that missing document, it was impossible for me to provide it, dispute it, or prove they had it.

And so, because of one allegedly missing document, they closed my file. I begged them to just tell me what they were missing. I would provide it (if it even existed) and they could reopen my case.

They refused.

Instead, they again filed a foreclosure action. My first phone call with the Mr. Stevens did not start off well. He rather jovially said, "Well, here we are again!" If I had been in the room with him rather than on the phone, I think I would have slapped him (well, probably not really. I'm not a physically violent person).

I pointed out that we were "here again" because *his client* was refusing payments. I noted that *his client* had closed my file without notification, and that it was *his client* who was refusing to disclose which document allegedly was missing. I had hoped that professional courtesy might encourage him to push the bank a bit to work with me, but I saw none of that. I can only hope that karma will show up in this man's life at some point.

Ethical rules prohibit attorneys from talking to opposing parties without the consent of their counsel, but since I was the "party" in this case, I could still work with the bank directly. But because they had closed my file, I was forced to begin all over again. Daunted doesn't even begin to describe how I felt at this point. And it was ironic, given that the bank's attorney had previously asked to leave the case open so that if we failed to comply, *they* wouldn't have to "start over."

Did I mention that I have trouble letting go?

I began pressing the bank for a new agreement, but they refused to propose one, telling me they were "swamped." Although I could be completely wrong, my opinion is that they had closed the file for a sham reason (if it wasn't false, why wouldn't they tell me which document they were missing?) and then refused to offer another agreement, because that's how I had "beaten" them the first time. If the bank was determined not to lose this time, it would not *give* me a proposal. The reasoning goes thus: If I didn't *have* an agreement, I couldn't *comply* with the agreement. No one ever *told* me this, of course; it's just my conjecture.

And then they refused to return my calls. From my perspective, it appeared they were no longer even bothering to *pretend* they were going to work with me.

The hearing on the second foreclosure was with a different judge, and not a particularly compassionate one. As my husband and I waited in the courtroom, another attorney that I knew came out of the judge's chambers. Oh, no—please, no. I made small talk and prayed he wouldn't ask me why I was there. He must have sensed my distress, because although it's a standard question among attorneys while waiting in the courtroom for the judge, he did not ask.

Despite having been in numerous courtrooms for various types of hearings, this one was obviously different. It was personal. I got a little taste of the anxiety my clients must have felt every time they had to go into a courtroom. I'm not sure whether it was worse for them (because a courtroom is a foreign experience for most) or for me (because of the shame factor in front of colleagues). I *do* know that my heart was pounding, and I wanted to be almost any-where but there.

And then the judge called me back to his chambers. After em-phasizing the fact that we had been compliant throughout the previous agreement and that the *bank* had refused payments, I ex-plained that the bank claimed I was missing a document but re-fused to tell me what it was. When I showed the judge the stack of documents I had *already* provided to the bank, his eyes grew wide. I felt encouraged, sure that he would understand the ludicrous-ness of closing a file that had been open for going on two years at that point simply because of *one* document—that might not even exist! I argued to the court common sense and basic fairness. You cannot *reject* payments and then foreclose because someone is not *making* payments.

But apparently you can.

On December 23, 2011 (Merry Christmas, right?), the court issued its order permitting the bank to foreclose on our home. When I pulled the envelope from the mailbox, my heart began to race. I was shaking so bad, I could barely open the door to get back in the house. Our very future was contained in this envelope. Had the court agreed with me? Or had it taken the side of the bank?

Opening the order, I did what any attorney would have done— I skipped to the very last page to see what the official decision was. And I felt physically ill. I went back to the beginning and read the whole opinion, trying to make sense of it. Although I understand *what* the judge ordered, to this day, I still do not understand *why* he granted the bank's foreclosure action.

Did I mention I have trouble letting go?

There was still a six-month delay of sale, supposedly so we could still try to work with the bank to save our home. However, in February, in yet another example of "kick us when we're down," my husband lost the job he had held for fifteen years and was not gainfully employed again until mid-April.

For the bank to work with us, it required a complete packet of documents. Keep in mind, they already *had* all the documents they were requesting, with one exception. A full packet for the bank included paystubs. Since Randy had lost his job, he didn't *have* any paystubs, which meant we could not submit a full packet until mid-May when he was again gainfully employed and had gone through at least two pay cycles. It finally became apparent, even to me, that despite the bank's positive sounding statements, they had no intention of working out a solution with us, so I hired a realtor to sell the home.

I prayed that it would sell within 10 days of the listing. It was a rather arbitrary number, but since we were getting so close to that six-month deadline, we didn't have the luxury of time. Miraculously, on the ninth day, we had not one but two offers, one of which was cash. *Two* offers, during one of the worst housing markets ever. We accepted the non-cash offer (it was first, it was higher, and it was pre-approved), subject, of course, to the bank's approval (since it was a short-sale). For the first time in a long time, I felt like I could breathe. A short-sale wasn't ideal, but it was a heck of a lot better than a foreclosure/sheriff's sale.

And there *was* a sheriff's sale scheduled for August 2, 2012. The buyers wanted to close on August 17, a mere *15 days* after the scheduled sale, for a property that had been tied up in foreclosure for over three years at this point, with literally *no payments* being made for eight months, and reduced payments prior to that. But in a move that stunned our realtor, the bank refused to approve the sale, choosing instead to let it go to sheriff's sale. It felt like they were determined to punish us for daring to fight to keep our home instead of rolling over and just letting them have it, no matter what it cost *them*.

Because of the way the judge wrote the December order, the mortgage was to transfer "immediately," so I believed, based upon what my realtor told me, that we needed to be out *that day*. Trying to find a new place to live, packing up and moving out of our house of 13 years in less than a week goes down as the second most ex-cruciatingly painful week of my life. I had tried to reassure myself that if we absolutely couldn't find something, we could always go to an extended stay hotel for a few weeks and put our things in a storage unit.

Except that we couldn't. The Iowa State Fair was that week, and there were "no vacancies in the inns." That last, final struggle about did me in. And again, Randy was working a new job that demanded *many* hours. He was not able to help me look or even figure out a solution. This was a battle I had largely fought on my own from start to bitter finish. Alone and isolated hardly begins to describe how I felt. Because I was the lawyer, and I was the one who wasn't working, I was, by default, the one to handle it.

In the end, no one won. It was nearly two years from the time the bank rejected that first payment to the sale of the property (six *months* after the sheriff's sale. Over two years with *no money* being paid. The cost of the bank's little power play was thousands of dollars, not including the attorney fees. And if they had allowed us to do the short sale, they would have sold the property for over $15,000 more than they eventually did. And I'm sure our former neighbors were thrilled to have the house sit empty for that length of time.

You hang on to things too long, which causes significantly more pain when they finally "leave" (or, in this case, are forcibly removed from my life). Sigh.

I fought and fought to keep my house, when I should have sold it much sooner. I couldn't let go because we built the house—doing much of the work ourselves. Memories of hanging siding and drywall, painting and doing the finish electrical work made the house more *ours* than if we had just bought an existing home. People that we cared about, some of whom were no longer living, had helped us build our home.

My cousin and his son had laid the carpet, friends helped us drywall the 17-foot ceiling and another friend did the finish carpentry. We watched deer run across the field while hanging siding, and there were the inevitable "injury stories" that accompany many projects like this. You know—the ones that are scary and painful when they happen, but that become a humorous part of family lore when retold.

We had raised our children in this house—birthday parties, Halloween parties and family gatherings. Baking days at Christmas, graduation celebrations and sitting in front of the fireplace with a glass of wine and a good book. School lessons and life lessons and everything in between. How could I sell the place where all that had transpired?

But if I had set aside the raw emotions for even a brief period, I would have realized that we could no longer afford the house. At that point, we would have two choices: either let go of it on *our* terms, or the bank's terms. If we had let go of it on our terms, we might still have had to do a short sale (it was the time of the housing crisis, after all), but our financial life wouldn't have taken as big a hit as it did with the foreclosure and sheriff's sale. And instead of spending those three years fighting to keep the house, we could have begun rebuilding our credit and moving forward. We might even be in a new home of our own by now.

But I simply refused to see that at the time. I refused to let go.

It *was* excruciatingly painful to have the house taken from us the way it was. Yet even after it went to sheriff's sale, I planned to file a complaint with the attorney general's office. They advised me that since the house had already been lost to a sheriff's sale, they really couldn't help me. The point wasn't to help *me*; it was to help *others* not have to go through that. But then I heard that voice whispering, *Let it go.* I realized that continuing the fight was just another way of trying to hold on to it.

As an aside, I would note that as painful as all this was, *telling* people—especially our kids and our siblings—was equally difficult. *What respectable people lose their house?* I thought. But not once did anyone blame us or offer anything other than straight-up love and support. Our children, Kierra and Logan, were adults and living on their own, but both returned to help. Randy's older brother Jeff, his wife Pam and their son James also came and helped.

I remember laying on the living room floor with Kierra after all the furniture had been moved out. Although carpeted, the room had an eerie, echoing quality to it, as though the house knew it was empty and was about to be abandoned. The lamps cast strange shadows on the walls because there was nothing to catch the light. Kierra and I were taking a break and having a discussion about, of all things, elbows. It was a random moment of wacky humor that was a welcome relief amidst all the sorrow and loss.

My friends Lori and Terri checked in via text all week, and especially on moving day, asking how I was. And my son, Logan, was particularly protective and solicitous of me. As we began running out of time and running out of space in the truck, it became clear to me that there were certain things that were going to be left behind. But Logan insisted that if there was something I wanted to take, we would make sure it found a way on the truck. He was not willing to accept "this will have to be left behind."

After we moved to our condo, my brother and his family came to visit. He took one look at me and said, "You look way more relaxed." I had not realized how the stress of fighting over the house had affected everything, even how I looked. I certainly wasn't happy about the outcome, but at least it was *done*. There was nothing more to fight about. It was over. I had no choice but to physically let it go. Now it was time to let it go emotionally so I could move on.

CHAPTER 2
THE MENTOR

When I started working in the financial industry in 2010, my default mentor was a man named Mason. Mason had originally viewed me as a potential client, but when that didn't work out, he switched gears and recruited me as a financial representative. I had been trying to build my business, but coming out of the crash of 2008, that wasn't going well. Mason painted a scenario where I could work as much or as little as I wanted as a financial representative, while continuing to build my business. Another attraction was that I could finally get the financial education I was so sorely lacking.

Unfortunately, the scenario he painted wasn't exactly the way things worked out. The restrictions on "other business" were significant, especially regarding the type of business I was trying to do. Compliance wanted to control what I said, how I marketed myself and so forth. Although they never said I *couldn't* do the other things I was working on, they made it so onerous that it was virtually impossible.

But I still needed the financial education, so I set aside my dreams of my own consulting business for a while and settled into my new professional home. I passed the insurance exams in record time, and I later passed my Securities 6/63 exam on the first try as well. I sat in on a few meetings with Mason, but it didn't take long for me to realize that although I didn't dislike him, he was not going to be a good fit for me as a mentor. I wanted to move faster than he was willing to let me.

I remember asking if I could run a client meeting after I had observed him run one a number of times. Rather than suggest I "practice" with him, he said, "Whoa—you've got to walk before you can run." In other words, *I* was ready to take on more responsibility, but he wasn't willing to relinquish it. I knew we were going to have to part ways if I was going to learn as fast as I wanted to. So I began coming up with reasons to justify that separation.

In the area of family law, Iowa is a no-fault divorce state (stay with me here—I promise I will connect the dots). You don't have to have a reason, beyond stating that there has been a "breakdown of the marriage relationship to the extent that the legitimate objects of matrimony have been destroyed and there remains no reasonable likelihood that the marriage can be preserved" (yes, that exact language had to actually appear in the pleading and the decree). Which is just a fancy way of saying, "We don't want to be married anymore."

Generally speaking, I agree with no-fault divorce, because before that, people who simply didn't want to be married any longer would have to lie—sometimes collaboratively—to get divorced. It caused more acrimony and was harder on the kids. It's not that no-fault divorce is easier, per se, but rather that you don't have to be so *creatively dishonest* about your reasons for wanting it.

At this point, you're probably wondering when, exactly, I will connect the dots between Iowa "family law" and letting go of my default mentor. Here it is: I don't like to be seen as the "bad guy." I will take responsibility for my actions, yet at the same time, I feel the need to justify those actions. So rather than take the no-fault way out, I always feel the need to explain my decision so that people don't think badly about me. And while I don't manufacture those reasons (i.e., lie), my "vision" becomes a spectacular 20/20 when I'm looking for reasons.

I'm simply going to say that I needed to let go of Mason as a mentor, (which was the easy part) *and* my need to justify that decision (which was the much harder part).

Even though I didn't want to continue working with Mason, I still needed *a* mentor if I was going to have any chance of succeeding in this business because it was so totally foreign to me. I had a degree in elementary education and a law degree—neither of which prepared me for a career in finance. And for personal reasons, I needed to learn as quickly as possible, as the previous chapter suggests.

As an aside, you might wonder why anyone would hire a financial advisor who had gone through foreclosure, but I would first say that no one ever asked what *my* financial world looked like. And even if they had, there is a certain logic to working with someone who can help you avoid the mistakes she has made.

Yet it is a difficult place from which to operate. Although I could blame my financial troubles on ignorance (I had never learned the principles I now knew), and although almost no one I worked with knew of my struggles, it was still awkward in my mind. I wanted a mentor who could help me excel, to overcompensate for my personal financial failures.

Shortly after I started, I began hearing about the guy who ran the Cedar Falls office. Curt had been in the business for many years, had unquestionable integrity and values and had mentored two other top producers. I decided it was time to pay him a visit.

It turned out to be one of the strangest meetings I've ever had—in a good way. When I first entered the office, there was a small sign on the front desk welcoming me. I have to say I have never—before or since—had a meeting where they took the time to put out a welcome sign! It was a small thing, but it made a big impression.

And the books! Even in the reception area, there were books. I pulled out one on leadership and began to read. When Curt came out to get me, I started to put the book back, but he stopped me. He told me to keep it, to finish reading it and return it when I was finished.

Once in his office, we began talking. I was used to meetings where the other person talked most of the time, but because Curt rarely does what other people do, he spent more time listening. I remember he perked up a bit when he discovered I was familiar with the *Clifton Strengthsfinder Assessment,* as it was something he used regularly in his own practice. But it felt like I was doing all the talking. I can only imagine (probably incorrectly) what he was thinking at the end of that meeting!

But as I look back, I sometimes wish I had the guts to ask him what it was about that meeting that piqued his interest, causing him to be willing to take me on as a "student." What did he see that made him think I was worth his time, busy as he was?

Of course, that first meeting didn't automatically result in the mentoring relationship that ultimately developed.

Both the Des Moines office and the Cedar Falls office had Monday morning meetings. In Des Moines, they were mandatory. Every meeting seemed to have the same theme: how to sell more life insurance. Don't misunderstand—life insurance is crazy important for people to have. It can mean the difference between survival and disaster for a family. But in this office, the focus was on using the numbers to sell the product, and making sure we knew how to run all the hypotheticals and use the software. I had heard very different stories about the meetings in Cedar Falls, and decided I wanted to go to those instead. So I asked Curt if I could attend his meetings instead of the ones in Des Moines.

He looked at me for a minute and said, "Well, you can attend one and never come again, or you can come every week. But you cannot drop in and out." I told him I understood. He probably thought I wouldn't show—Cedar Falls is a four-hour round trip drive, after all, for a two-hour meeting. That's a lot of drive time to invest *every week*, especially in Iowa in the winter. But I did show up. If he was surprised, he didn't show it. And I continued to show up, week after week, not because I had to, but because the meetings provided such *value* to me as a new representative.

The rumors I had heard were true: the meetings in Cedar Falls *were* very different. Those meetings were focused on serving people and on building relationships. They were high-octane meetings, fueled by passion to do the very best work. They were competitive in a *good* way—the goal was always to come up with the best solution for the client.

They were fast paced, with incredible participation, and there was a great deal of trust, which allowed a lot of pushback without egos getting in the way. Everyone there, from the support staff to the other advisors, was willing to help me and answer questions. These meetings created such a strong bond that when we had meetings incorporating all the offices, I sat with "my" Cedar Falls guys instead of my home office Des Moines people.

After the official Monday morning meeting, which lasted a couple hours, a group of us (most of us, in fact), would head over to a Mexican restaurant for $1 tacos. There was one guy, though, who consistently declined, saying he didn't really like their tacos. I looked at him, smiled and said, "Jim! It's not about the tacos!" And it wasn't.

Lunch was where the conversations continued. And on some Mondays, Curt would work with me on some of my cases after that. There are not too many people who can make my head explode, but he fed me information so fast that the two-hour return trip to Des Moines felt like a blink of an eye, so immersed was I in processing everything he had taught me. Good thing it was an easy drive on a four-lane highway! It was like not only drinking from a fire hose, but a fire hose filled with caffeine—and I *loved* it!

Curt is the consummate teacher, and Learner is one of my strengths (under the aforementioned *Strengthsfinder Assessment*). This meant that the more Curt taught me, and the more he and his "gang" in Cedar Falls challenged me, the happier I was. I remember having lunch with him one day after a meeting. I was still pretty new, so if there was something in the meeting I didn't understand, I didn't always speak up in the group meeting—I waited until I could ask Curt. He would patiently explain it to me until I got it.

On this day, I said, "I didn't understand that part Todd was talking about regarding borrowing from your life insurance contract." I explained where my confusion was, and he grabbed a napkin, pulled his Pilot G-2 blue pen (it's a strategy) out of his pocket, and writing upside down (*another* strategy), diagrammed it out for me.

I still didn't understand. "Tell me that again," I said. He did. And suddenly, I got it! I was so excited I nearly bounced out of my seat. The proverbial light bulb had exploded above my head, and Curt beamed. I'm not sure who was more pleased.

But after a few years, I realized that although I loved the learning and the teaching and the strategic part of the business (strategic is another strength of mine), I did *not* love the marketing and compliance pieces. Even though I was a lawyer, making the compliance part perhaps easier for me than others, it still drove me crazy. Compliance in the legal world was a piece of cake compared to compliance in the financial world.

I remember one document I submitted for approval to the compliance department. It was a marketing piece, and I had carefully worded it to ensure it would be approved the first time through. And it almost was, except for one word they wanted me to change. Now, in the financial world, you couldn't just change it and send it out. They needed to see it again, *even though* they *gave me* the word they wanted me to use instead. So I dutifully submitted the change to the same compliance person.

Unbelievably, he returned it, telling me *that* word was not acceptable. Well, that warranted a phone call, not an email. So I called him and said in frustration, "Hey, that word that I changed, that you said was not acceptable? That was *your* word! *You* gave me that word!" He laughed ruefully and said, "I know. But after I thought about it…"

This is the kind of thing that drives me crazy, and it made me realize that this was not my calling, or even the best use of my strengths, talents and gifts. Yet I stayed long beyond that realization. I wouldn't let it go. Why? Part of my hesitation to change professions has to do, again, with my loyalty. This time, however, I was looking for reasons to leave the *industry,* not the person. I didn't want to disappoint Curt, or to make him feel like he had wasted his time with me. He spent so much of his valuable time coaching me and teaching me, and now I was going to quit.

My friend Susan listened to all my anxiety and made a very insightful comment. She simply said, "Maybe that's not why he's in your life."

That caught me up short, and it brought back a long forgotten memory. Several years before that, I had asked God for a mentor. Not just any mentor, mind you, but someone I dubbed a "life mentor." Most mentors helped you with the professional work you were doing, but I was looking for someone to more broadly mentor me—someone to talk to me about faith and values, relationships and decisions to be made along life's journey.

Because my dad died when I was very young, and my mom and I were so different, I never really felt like I had this kind of life mentoring. I had made this plea for a very long time. But the right person never showed up, so I quit asking and eventually forgot about my dream. I was on my own in this world, which is a very lonely place to be.

I had also asked for someone who would teach me about money. I assumed that this money person would be in the form of a financial planner. I never would have dreamed of learning about money in the way it showed up—from a mentor rather than advisor. But it truly was the best way for me to benefit from his tremendous knowledge and expertise (and just plain good advice generally).

Susan's observation reminded me of those long forgotten prayers and helped me see that both prayers had been answered in one person. Curt *wasn't* just in my life to teach me about money (although he did that brilliantly). I realized that he was the life mentor I had prayed for all those years ago. In fact, God had *over-blessed* me in this area. And I think that, intuitively, that's the real reason I was afraid of quitting the financial job—I was afraid I would lose his guidance and his insight.

As it turns out, he's not *just* a financial coach (and I'm still not a client). In fact, our discussions now are rarely about financial issues. Instead, we talk about leadership, business, faith and values. Curt is a person who walks his talk and integrates his faith and values into everything he does, whether people realize it or not. I never question his integrity or his intention. That's not to say that I always agree with him or his positions. But even when I disagree, I still benefit because it makes me think a little harder about why I believe what I do.

There was a lot of letting go here: letting go of my default mentor, my need to find "reasons" to justify my decisions so I don't look like the bad guy, and my position as a financial advisor (although compliance said I wasn't technically allowed to call myself that). But thankfully, I did *not* have to let go of having Curt as a mentor.

At least not at that point.

CHAPTER 3

FEAR

Yesterday afternoon, I was having a rather choppy phone conversation with my mentor as he drove back to Cedar Falls (he was, apparently, in that well-known "dead zone" on Highway 20). I had been working on a different chapter of this book, one about letting go of the need to see the whole staircase before taking even the first step, and was thinking about how different I was in high school and college. I thought about the way Curt tried to live his life, holding on loosely to things. I had apparently forgotten how to do that, if I ever really knew how. So I just asked him. "How do you do that?"

I suspect those out-of-the-blue questions I occasionally fire off catch him off guard, although he never lets on if they do. He paused thoughtfully for a moment, but instead of answering, asked me a question.

"What are you afraid of?"

Do you remember *A Charlie Brown Christmas*? Where Lucy, playing the role of psychologist, "analyzes" Charlie Brown, seeking to find out what *he's* afraid of? She names several phobias and then asks him if he thinks he has pantaphobia. When she tells him that pantaphobia means the fear of everything, he exclaims, "That's it!"

toppling her off her stool. Well, that's a little how I feel at times, although I didn't say that to Curt yesterday.

He went on to remind me that when we're afraid, we hold on to things too tightly. I told him that I hadn't always been this way. I was more confident, more sure of myself and had loads more *fun* back in high school and college. Now, Curt didn't know me back then, of course, so I had to fill him in a bit. I ended by telling him that I liked myself a lot better in high school and college than I do now. Which wasn't exactly accurate. What I *meant* was, I liked my *life* better back then; I wasn't worried and afraid all the time. But I wasn't sure how to get back to the girl I was "back then."

Now, it's not that I was *never* afraid in high school or college—it just didn't *control* my life the way it sometimes does now. I learned early on that my response to fear—real or otherwise—was not fight or flight, but was instead the recently acknowledged freeze.

When I was in high school, both my boyfriend and I had jobs that kept us working late. He was an assistant manager at a theater, and I was a waitress at a pizza parlor. He would often come over after we both got off work, but one evening, as I pulled into the driveway, I didn't see where he parked, so didn't think he was there yet. I lived on a corner, and the driveway was behind the house. Jon had parked in the front, in the neighboring business's driveway. He went in through the front gate and was sitting on the porch swing, waiting for me when I came around the corner. I saw Jon, but in the dark, I didn't initially recognize that it was him. And since I didn't see his car, I assumed he wasn't there yet. I thought there was a stranger sitting on the swing.

I froze. I could not have been more paralyzed if I had suffered a full-blown stroke. And once I realized it was Jon, my paralysis terrified me even more. What if he had been a *real* threat?

But it's not just the threat of real (or perceived) *physical* danger that causes me to freeze. It's the fear of making a mistake, of choosing "wrong." It's the fear of losing things or people that I love. It's the fear of never having enough. It's the fear of wasting all the gifts God has generously given me. But in order to use those gifts, I have to run the risk of making mistakes, of being wrong.

It's even possible that people I care about won't like what I write and will "unfriend" me (okay, that's not just a possibility—that's actually happened). And what if the naysayers are right, whether about my personal life or my ability to earn a living as a writer? What if I *can't* make money writing? Thankfully, a little voice speaks up and says, "But what if you *can?*"

And so I try.

As I recounted in the introduction, the first book I submitted to my editor received a rather lukewarm response. After praying about it, I realized I sent the wrong book. But the "right" book was – is – very challenging to write and publish. I asked myself what I was hoping to achieve by publishing this book. I sat quietly, reflecting on how this book would potentially change my life and whether I was brave enough to take that leap. I remembered my theme for the year, one that had been "percolating" for a few years—*Be Strong and Courageous.* I first heard this Joshua Prayer at the Global Leadership Summit in 2013, but it continued to show up in rather odd places and times. For example, when I was praying about whether I should keep writing, this version of the prayer showed up for me in 2 Chronicles: "Be Strong and courageous *and do the work.*"

So I kept writing. But in December of 2014, I was getting impatient. The verse showed up again, a bit differently. I was selected to be a reader for our church's *Lessons and Carols* service, and the verse assigned to me was from Psalms: "Be strong and courageous and *wait* on the Lord."

I remembered during one of my quiet meditation times receiving the message, *You can help a lot of people.* Although some might find my tips and techniques from the "safe" book to be helpful, this scary book had the potential to help many, many more people on a much more fundamental level. It would help people see they weren't alone. It could help *them* let go of the things that were holding them back.

And then I remembered a dream I had a few years back. I was carrying a baby named Grace in my arms, when a huge storm approached. Being an Iowa girl, I headed to the basement with baby Grace. When the storm was over, I came upstairs to see that my former house was gone. In its place was the most beautiful home I could imagine, surrounded by beautiful countryside and filled with everything my heart could desire. Blessing after blessing.

When homes appear in our dreams, they typically signify our lives. What this dream said to me was that I would go through a big "storm" in my life but that, by grace, I would come out of it stronger, leading the life I had always dreamed of. Even if this book caused a big storm, I decided to be strong and courageous and publish it, hoping for grace when called for.

I set a calendar appointment with my editor to make sure I did the work and didn't chicken out (which I really, really wanted to do). The very next day I came across a blog post about "10 Harsh Truths that Might Be Holding You Back," and almost every one of them had the phrase "let it go" in it—the original title of my book. And every one of them could serve as a chapter.

This hasn't been an easy process. I had to be strong and courageous in my conversations and relationships *before* the book was published. I had to relive painful memories in order to write about them (and yes, I cried some). And I had to be willing to accept that some people might not want to be friends if they knew the "real" me, even though that had not been my experience with the loss of my house. When I told close friends what had happened, not one of them criticized or abandoned me. They were compassionate and supportive. I would have to trust that the people I cared about most would not abandon me when the book came out.

To be sure, I am not a violent criminal (or even a non-violent one). I have not been cursed with substance abuse problems, poor health or been a victim of domestic violence. My problems likely seem small compared to those of others. But when they're *your* problems, they never seem small to you. To paraphrase Dr. Phil, just because the guy next to you broke his leg doesn't mean your sprained ankle doesn't hurt.

Interestingly, my biggest self-created problems (e.g., losing my house and going to law school) have been around my biggest fear—not having enough money. I'm sure there's a sermon in that sentence somewhere, but I'm not ready to preach it quite yet.

In my conversation with Curt, he suggested that I return to a childlike trust in God. But what does that mean, exactly? I thought of a missing child alert I had recently seen on Facebook. People were frantically looking for this little boy, and one woman even said she had seen him on the corner of a very busy street (but didn't realize he was "missing" at the time).

Ultimately, he was found—and was safe. He had not been kidnapped—he was running away from a bad home situation. A *fifth grader* was running away from home. Where did he think he was going? How was he going to get there? How would he take care of himself in the meantime? It apparently never occurred to him to worry about the next step. It was the ultimate in child-like faith to believe that everything would turn out for the best, even if he didn't know quite *how* that would look.

I'm not sure I'm ready for that level of childlike faith. Maybe I should be, but I'm not. I tread carefully along that narrow line between faith and foolishness. It's getting better, though. With each chapter I turn over to my editor (and her encouraging and positive feedback), I feel stronger. For the first time in a very long time, I feel like I'm exactly where I'm supposed to be, profession-ally speaking. I'm not trying to plan out the whole process, instead choosing to trust that the people and the resources I need will show up when I need them.

And here's an interesting little twist: A funny thing happened when I was looking up the exact phobia Lucy diagnosed for Charlie Brown. It turns out she misdiagnosed him. Pantaphobia doesn't mean the fear of everything. It really means the fear of *nothing*.

Could I somehow get closer to living out *that* diagnosis?

CHAPTER 4
THE KIDS

Although no one is a perfect parent, I think that by and large I have done a good job with my kids. Do I have regrets, things I could have done differently? Sure—that's normal. But if I look at the big picture, there are really only two questions: Did I love them to the best of my ability, and are they responsible, independent adults? The answer to both of those questions is a resounding "Yes." Does that mean they always make the choices I think they should? Of course not. But they're adults now; they get to make their own decisions.

I was fortunate to have one of those rare "validating" parent moments after Logan moved to Iowa City. He was living on his own quite successfully. He had a job, he was going to school and he was navigating adulthood with few problems. He returned home for a visit, and we went to Panera for lunch.

When my kids were in elementary and junior high school, we used to have "coffee" dates at a local Panera. I would take one or the other of them there, and we would have a beverage and a snack and just talk about what was going on in their life. These were the kinds of conversations that you don't have in the five-minute drive home from school, or even around the dinner table when everyone is there. These were more relaxed, and sometimes deeper. Other times, they were just filled with funny chatter that had no deep philosophical meaning. Heading to Panera with Logan when he returned from Iowa City reminded me of those earlier visits.

Logan is my intense child. He has always felt things acutely and expressed his opinions strongly (I have no *idea* who he gets that from!). I remember a time when he was in junior high and he came to talk to me about a history class he was taking. I am an early-to-bed person and had just turned out the light. Logan came in and started talking. He was literally all over the world map and the global calendar, connecting one dictator's actions to another. The ramifications of one war to future military actions. The consequences of unstable regions on future generations. He was trying so hard to have his words keep up with his thoughts that they just came *pouring* out of him. I could almost feel my hair blowing back from the sheer force of his thoughts and analysis.

This is one of those gifted kids things. And I wondered how much he was holding in on a daily basis because people just would not be able to keep up with him. He is sometimes underestimated because he is athletic (that kid can run for hours without tiring—I'm pretty sure he does *not* get that from me) and extraordinarily handsome. He can charm people into doing what he wants, but you probably don't want to cross him (and while my husband probably gets credit for the charming part, my family history suggests I likely have to own that last part).

But on this day at Panera, we were not having deep philosophical discussions. We were simply chatting and watching people cross the plaza to enter the mall when he suddenly looked at me and said out of the blue, "I am *so* glad you weren't a helicopter parent!" I burst out laughing and asked what prompted that comment.

He told me of an experience his friend Jacob had with *his* mother. Jacob had applied for a cashier's job at a store in the mall. He hadn't heard back from the store manager, so his mom urged him to follow up. Jacob resisted her advice, saying that they said they would call if they were interested.

Wanting to use this as a teachable moment, his mom talked to him about showing initiative, but he stood his ground and said he wasn't going to call. If she had left it there, there would have been no problem. But she unfortunately took her "helpfulness" a step too far a few days later.

Jacob, his mom and his sister happened to be shopping in this store, when his mom saw a manager. She urged Jacob to go talk to him, but Jacob again refused.

You can guess what happened next. *Mom* went and talked to the manager. Jacob begged her not to, but she was determined. She asked the manager why they hadn't called her son, and the manager politely explained that they don't hire college kids for the summer unless they have previously worked for them. It takes too long to train them, and then they leave to go back to school. They're looking for kids who can work year round, which is perfectly reasonable.

Mom finished the conversation by "suggesting" that it would be common courtesy to let these kids know instead of making them wait for a call that's never going to come. Keep in mind that Jacob had not had an interview; she was essentially asking the store to contact *every single person* who *applied* for a job.

Logan, in telling me the story, shook his head and said, "That company will *never* hire him." And he's right—not because Jacob is a college kid and unable to work year round. Not because he couldn't do the job well. No, this company will never hire Jacob because his mom intervened instead of letting him handle it. This is a mom who intervenes at every level, complaining about how teachers, employers and doctors are either too hard on her kids or aren't doing what they should—and then wonders why she's labeled a troublemaker, or why her kid struggles to get a job.

Personally, the closest I got to helicopter "status" was when Logan was in eighth grade. He was taking classes at Central Academy, a school for academically gifted kids. He had a science project that was to take several months to complete. Time passed, and he hadn't even started the project. As the deadline started looming, *I* became more agitated.

Finally, one night, when he was sitting upstairs *not* working on the assignment again, I said, "Logan! This project is due in *two weeks,* and you haven't even *started!*" I'm sure you can vividly imagine my tone of voice in this exchange! I lectured him about the virtues of being responsible. I told him that if the teacher gave them several months to complete the project it was because she expected it to *take* several months to complete. On and on I went, getting more worked up the more he did not respond.

Finally Logan had had enough. "I KNOW, MOM!" he shouted. And that stopped me in my tracks. I realized that he *did* know. He knew when it was due. He knew he hadn't started. He knew what his project was and how to do it. He *knew* all about it—he was simply choosing not to *do* anything about it.

So I took a deep breath and said to him (in a *much* calmer voice), "You're right. You do know. I won't say anything more about it. But if you need me to take you somewhere to get supplies (he wasn't old enough to drive yet), you need to give me enough notice to do that for you." In other words, I was putting him on notice that I was not going to drop everything to take him to the craft store at the last minute simply because he refused to stay on top of the project.

I'm here to tell you, my tongue was nearly *bleeding* from all the times I had to bite it in the next two weeks. He was clearly going to fail on this project. Not because he wasn't smart enough, but because he simply wasn't doing anything. Should I jump in, despite my promise to stay out of it? Should I threaten to ground him? I decided to simply keep my word (because integrity is a *really* high value of mine) and stay out of it, letting him feel the full consequences of his decision. Otherwise, we would go through this same exhausting process every time he had a big project due.

The night before the due date (I kid you not), he came into my bedroom as I was getting ready for bed and said in all seriousness, "I don't suppose you would call me in sick tomorrow, would you?"

I about came unglued on him! Fire shot from my eyes as I asked him, "Are you out of your *mind*? No, I will not call you in sick! You've had plenty of time to do this project and have chosen not to. You will go to school tomorrow, and you should expect to receive a grade commensurate with the level of effort you have put into it." And he did.

Lesson learned.

In my daughter's case, her big lesson came when she wanted to go to an Ivy League college for undergraduate school. I suggested she apply early and have her Advanced Placement teachers review her college essay. She did neither of those things. With the internet, you can apply *minutes* before the deadline and, assuming no technical issues, be fine. I tried to suggest that perhaps an early admission might improve her chances, given that most people *aren't* doing that. She declined, wanting to keep her options open. And she had her friends, rather than her AP English teacher, read her essay. Now, she is an exceptionally talented writer, and she has very bright friends, but they didn't know any more about writing a college essay than she did.

Kierra is so capable and so competent that she rarely "updated" me on what she was doing, choosing instead to figure it out and just do it. I would check in with her and ask how she was progressing, but she shared few details. Too many questions, and she would let me know through a look or her tone that she had it covered and I should stop asking so many questions.

My parents had never gone to college. I couldn't do online research about various colleges, and there were no businesses like the one my friend Tom Kleese owns that are designed to help kids choose—and get into—the best college *for them*. Because I had been to college (and law school), I thought Kierra would welcome my help and my insight. Hmmm…perhaps I had raised her to be a little *too* independent. Or perhaps I was simply delusional.

I also tried to encourage her to apply to a "gimme" school—the one that you can get into easily should your first choice(s) not pan out. She refused. She had her sights set on an Ivy League school, and nothing would dissuade her from that. She had *always* succeeded in any academic challenge she had ever faced, so she had no reason to think this would be any different. Although she had "diversified" her applications between various schools, they were still all top-tier schools.

People would try to reassure me, saying things like, "She's really smart—she'll get in." And she *is* really smart. She and Logan are both "wicked smart," as the saying goes. But I reminded the people saying this that *all* kids applying to those schools were smart; that wasn't enough. And some decisions are beyond the control of the students. If the school is looking to build its engineering department, for example, and your child isn't pursuing engineering, she might not get in, even if she is a stronger candidate overall.

Ultimately, she did not get in to any of the schools she had selected. When the last rejection letter came in, she cried, and my girl does not often cry. When she was a preschooler, the class took a field trip to the zoo. While looking at the monkeys from under a rail, she stood suddenly and cracked her head on the rail. That hurt, and she understandably cried. The preschool teachers looked around, puzzled. One finally said, "Is that *Kierra?* I don't think I've ever heard her cry."

I suspect that not getting in to her first-choice schools was even more painful than hitting her head at the monkey exhibit. I didn't say anything, just sat with her and rubbed her back, letting her cry. Could I have said, "I told you so?" Sure. But why would I say something so hurtful to someone I love so much? There was no triumph in being "right," and pointing out that she should have followed my advice would have been a breaking moment instead of a supportive, loving moment. And there is no guarantee that following my suggestions would have resulted in a different outcome, either.

It was painful for me to witness her grief over this lost opportunity, and a difficult lesson for her to learn. It's tough to watch your kids fail. But it's much better for them to fail as children or teenagers, when the consequences are typically less permanent. And if it's painful enough, they will avoid those consequences in future endeavors. But if you are constantly swooping in to rescue them, they will never learn to make good decisions themselves. Mistakes are how we grow and learn. Overcoming these mistakes is how kids (and adults) become more self-reliant and develop *true* self-confidence (rather than simply collecting "participation trophies").

The other interesting thing that came out of this is that my kids are much more willing to ask for my advice now.

The summer Logan was going to turn twenty-one (the legal drinking age), we went on a family vacation to the Lake of the Ozarks. My brother- and sister-in-law own a home there, and generously invite us down for a long weekend with them every summer. This particular year, Logan also brought his friend, Ed. Everyone but Logan was old enough to drink. His birthday was just a few short weeks away. We were out on the boat one morning, and I was sitting where I always love to sit—in the front, with the wind and the spray (I am a true water person). Logan approached and asked if I would mind if he ordered a drink when we stopped for lunch—an *alcoholic* drink.

He made his case and then waited for me to respond. I first told him that although he was *close* to being old enough to drink, the fact remained that he *wasn't* old enough to legally drink, so he would be breaking the law. I told him he would be putting himself and his server at risk (he was and is an outstanding server, so he could relate to this). After I finished wrapping up *my* case, I added this: "But you are an adult, and you get to make your own decisions now."

I am proud to say he did not try to order a drink. Good man.

I think he was willing to ask for my opinion because he knew that I was not going to insist he do things my way. I told him what I thought and then reminded him that he didn't have to do it my way. He very often will do what I suggest, but even when he doesn't, it's okay. He has considered my perspective and has made an *informed* decision to do it differently. And that's what being an adult is about. We don't share all the same values, haven't had the same experiences or are in exactly the same situations. So sometimes the decisions *will* be different—not wrong, necessarily, just different. And sometimes they *will* be wrong. But that's part of the learning process, too.

Ultimately, all things *do* work together for good. My daughter obtained her master's degree in International Development from a prestigious school in Washington, D.C.—her *first* choice this time. Logan moved to Denver last summer, planning out the move, making sure he had plenty of money in an emergency savings account and lining up employment. He lives life on his terms and makes good decisions based upon his values and goals. Both are responsible, independent and confident kids, and I am extraordinarily proud to be their mom.

Letting go of the role you have when your kids are little can be hard, but if they are going to be successful, productive adults, it's necessary. And in my experience, they end up coming back to you in a relationship that's even stronger. There's no longer the (previously necessary) power imbalance that exists between an adult parent and minor child, which allows an extremely rewarding adult relationship to develop.

And they might even thank you for not being a helicopter parent.

CHAPTER 5
KEEPING THE FAITH

I was born and raised a Methodist. My Irish grandfather was originally Catholic. But when he married my grandmother, he "moved over" to become a Methodist. At a certain point, my parents considered going "back" to being Catholic, though I'm not really sure what prompted that. My mother had been raised Baptist (no dancing in her household), so *she* didn't really have any ties to Catholicism.

Regardless of what caused them to consider the switch, here's how the story goes: My dad learned that, to be a Catholic, he would have to let his wife die if it came down to saving her or their baby in childbirth. Once he found that out, he put the kibosh on converting. I don't even know if that's a true "rule" in the Catholic Church, but that's the story I got. Heck, that *story* might not even be right, but that's my memory, faulty though it may (or may not) be.

I was raised in a smallish church on the east side of Des Moines called Sheridan Park United Methodist Church. We didn't live on the east side, and it always took us a good 30 minutes to get to church (taking the interstate was faster than going "through town"), but my dad had been raised on the east side, so that's where we went.

I have such fond memories of that church and the loving guidance I received there. Georgia Brown, a friend of my mom's, taught kindergarten, and every year her class sang *Away in the Manager* for the Christmas program, Georgia's voice warbling above the little 5-year-olds. She was a stout, no-nonsense woman with a big heart who loved her little kindergartners.

After the program, we would go down to the church hall and get a small treat bag. I was always optimistic that there would be something new and unique in that bag, but it inevitably included the mandatory candy cane and orange. Although I wasn't particularly impressed by the "gift" back then (I didn't like oranges as a child), it's funny how it became a part of a cherished memory.

In Sunday School, we memorized the books of the Bible. To this day, when I am trying to find a book in the New Testament, I sing the song we learned to memorize the order of the books. The Old Testament, though, was straight up memorization. We memorized Bible verses (the first being the much-loved John 3:16), and we sang *Do Lord, oh, Do Lord, oh, Do Remember Me,* and *I have the Joy, Joy, Joy, Joy, Down in my Heart*, with Jeanne Alfman enthusiastically leading us.

I remember singing out, and Jeanne laughing and saying, "Bless your heart." I thought she was making fun of me, and I sang more quietly after that. I realize now that the opposite was true; she was delighted by my own childish enthusiasm for music.

I became friends with Pam Wylie and Lisa Baker in my class, Colleen Jones and her brother Chris (Colleen one year older, Chris one year younger) and Rick Graham. I am still connected to *all* of these friends, even if it's just through Facebook.

Merle and Alice Marnin didn't have any biological kids, but every kid at that church was theirs. They both served the church in various capacities, but Alice's service stands out. She was the church secretary for *68 years*—retiring well after her ninetieth birthday! At her ninetieth birthday party, we took pictures of her and all the ministers she had "raised" in that church—and there were quite a few.

Alice called all of us "honey" (not because she couldn't remember our names—she could) and made sure we knew how much we were loved, although I can't recall anything specific that she did. It was just an overall feeling of being valued and cared for. She was one of my earliest models of Christian love and remains so even to this day. She is in her 90s but still cares deeply about her church family—even those of us who have moved on to other churches. Although I don't call the kids at my current church "honey," my model for speaking to them and *seeing* them is based on Alice Marnin's infallible method.

When I was an infant, Sheridan Park did not baptize babies, instead dedicating them to the church. Thus, when it came time to be confirmed, I had to first be baptized. My cousin, "Little" Larry (he wasn't little—it's just that his dad was Big Larry), and I both decided to be baptized by immersion, which meant we had to go to a different church to use its baptismal pool. It was a moving experience, made doubly so because of being baptized with my cousin. It required significant trust, because the minister leaned us *back* into the water. We had to rely on him to hold us and bring us back up. Being old enough to *choose* both the act and method of baptism (as well as being old enough to remember it) was deeply meaningful.

The minister at Sheridan Park also served a very small church called Capitol Heights UMC. Reverend Henry was not the first minister I had, but he was the first one I remember. When he was transferred to a different congregation (which occurred every seven years or so in the Methodist Church in those days), Capitol Heights had an additional challenge: *Mrs.* Henry had played piano for their services, but she would obviously be leaving as well. So in my sixteenth year of life, I became the pianist at Capitol Heights, earning the princely sum of $10/week. There might have only been about 15 people in the church on any given Sunday, but they were appreciative. The church was often *very* cold in the winter, and I remember shivering and wearing gloves between hymns to try to keep my fingers warm so I could play.

My mom would drop me off at Capitol Heights. I would play for their service, and then ride over to Sheridan Park with the minister. I remember that being a *very* long ride, as he, a father of two boys, struggled to make small talk with a teenaged girl he really didn't know—week after week. And then I had to listen to the sermon all over again.

Although this man probably cared for his congregation, his sermons were dry as unbuttered toast, and having to sit through them *twice* was a challenge, especially if I had worked my other job the evening before. When I got to college and took the all too common "sabbatical" from church, I explained that I had "banked" extra services for several years and was simply cashing in those deposits.

After marriage and the birth of my first child, I started going to church again. We landed at Walnut Hills, which became our church home for the next 18 years. It was a wonderfully welcoming church, and I was quite active there, happily serving in music, on boards and in classrooms. Leaving Walnut Hills was excruciating. Having been a Methodist all my life, it was difficult for me to contemplate a different denomination on top of changing churches, but I eventually did move to the United Church of Christ at Plymouth Congregational Church—or Plymouth Church, as most of us refer to it.

Like Walnut Hills, there is a great sense of community. At the end of every service, the congregation sings a benediction. The choir surrounds us, and you can see people swaying as they sing, in the same way they do when comforting a child or lulling a baby to sleep. It has such a feeling of connection—whether you know the person next to you or not—and often leaves me choked up, unable to sing.

Throughout this book, I talk about letting go of things, or at least holding loosely. This chapter is a reminder that there are some things, like my faith, that are worth holding on to—tightly. But I have to be careful about what, specifically, I am holding on to. It isn't about a specific church or denomination.

As author Christine Caine notes, "Jesus did not die so that we could have a religious belief system—but rather a life-giving relationship with our Father." I *have* let go of different churches and even denominations, for a variety of reasons. What I have held on to, and what has been most meaningful to me, is the *relationship* I have with God, one that transcends membership in a particular church. The church is in a unique position to create *opportunities* for relationship—both with God and other people—which, in my opinion, is one of its greatest values. But it doesn't *replace* faith and a personal relationship with God.

Reflecting on my time at Sheridan Park and the friendships I made there reminds me of a couple things that aren't always talked about: the church is instrumental in teaching values, and it also plays a large role in developing relationships and community.

Reconnecting with my church friends, especially Pam, has reinforced the belief that the friendships we forged in Sunday School, under the watchful eye of our church "village," were incredibly influential in shaping my character. Those relationships, along with my family ones, taught me right from wrong. The people in church were the ones who were there when my dad died. Our church friends stepped in and took my brother fishing and my family to ballgames. In short, they demonstrated God's love beyond the church's four walls.

I do not take that blessing lightly.

I know that not everyone holds tightly to faith. For some people, going to church is a routine, but not ritual; it's an obligation. Other people say they believe in God, but they have no particular relationship with Him. Others are quite upfront about saying they don't even believe in God—usually because they have either had no teaching or bad teaching regarding God. This has less to do with God and more with "religion."

But for me, I can't imagine a life without faith. My relationship with God is an anchor for me. It is a constant, when nothing else in life is, which is why I choose to hold tightly to that relationship, even as I hold loosely to church.

CHAPTER 6

BOARD MEMBERS

It's funny how the silliest, most seemingly insignificant things can pop up in your life years later and create a completely new bond.

When I was in college at The University of Northern Iowa (Go, Panthers!), my college roommate and I would sometimes go to the library together. Sleep-deprived college students that we were, it was hard to resist the siren song of sleep in the mostly silent library. Dee and I had to find a *quiet* way to stay awake.

Enter atomic fireballs.

Dee's neighbor from back home kept her stocked, but in case you have missed this particular delicacy, it is a small red candy that packs a wallop in terms of heat. They are a hard candy—a fiery red cinnamon outer shell with a sweet white core. They're big enough to make you look like a squirrel preparing for winter when you tuck them in your cheek. It's always a bit of a Russian Roulette though—sometimes you'll get a relatively mild one, and other times you'll get one that will make your eyes water until you absolutely *must* pop it out of your mouth and chug a glass of ice water. Other than the gasping, they were a perfectly quiet way to stay awake.

After college, I largely forgot about atomic fireballs. They're not really something you want to be eating in the courtroom, the classroom or a business meeting. I wasn't as sleep deprived (until I became a mother, that is, but I sense that atomic fireballs might not be a great thing to pass along to a nursing infant, so they weren't quite as good a solution as they were in college). And then they showed up in my life again in a totally unexpected, terrifically fun way.

I was at the point where I was strongly considering asking Curt to be my mentor. Oddly enough, I don't remember the first time I met him. I had heard of him, of course, in the "stuff of a legend" kind of way, but he was in the Cedar Falls office, two hours away, so I hadn't yet met him. My default mentor had sung Curt's praises, so I went to his website and looked at his picture—and was surprised. Dressed in a suit and tie (which I have *never* seen him wear in real life), I thought, *THIS is the guy who's so good? Who has such a unique approach? He looks like a stereotypical insurance salesman!*

I could not have been more wrong. Let me assure you, Curt is not a stereotypical *anything.* One time when he was talking to me on the phone while he was driving, he spotted a purple Dodge Charger and said he'd like to have one. I laughed and said, "Because purple is one of UNI's colors?"

"No," he responded. "Because no one else has one."

He is predictably *un*predictable. I don't know if he drinks Dos Equis beer, but he could give that guy in the commercial a run for his money in the "most interesting" category, because he simply never (well, almost never) does what you think he's going to.

But I digress.

When I realized that my default mentor was not going to work out, I decided I needed to learn more about Curt. At that same time, another woman in my office, Melinda, was also looking to him as a potential mentor. However, Melinda was rather manipulative, and it started feeling like a competition.

Curt was coming to Des Moines for the day, and Melinda had asked if he would meet with her. He agreed, but also suggested that I join them. My office was on an interior corner, and I could generally hear people coming down the hall, even before I could see them. I could hear Curt talking to Melinda, and I heard her say, "Well, Jean might not be here." I rolled my eyes and sighed. We had a meeting scheduled—why would I *not* be there?

When they came around the corner, Melinda feigned surprise and said, "Oh, you *are* here!" I largely ignored the comment, greeted Curt cheerfully and followed them to Melinda's office. She sat behind her desk, and Curt and I sat opposite her. She tried to direct the conversation, but that was short-lived—it became quickly apparent who was going to run that meeting! Curt has a laser-like focus and an incredible mind for strategic process, so he changed the direction of her conversation. But Curt doesn't *tell* people what to think; he simply asks a lot of questions. And you have to be quick to keep up with him.

While there's no way to be totally prepared for all the questions he might ask, I did know that I had to be at the top of my game and had reviewed some of my notes from previous meetings with him. And it was a good thing I did. I don't remember exactly what he asked, but he asked *me* a series of questions (rather than just generally throwing them out), all based on things he had already taught me. It felt like a pop quiz, but when I finished, he reached in his pocket, pulled out *an atomic fireball,* and slid it across the desk to me.

My eyes grew large, and I exclaimed, "I *love* these things!"

Little did I know that they were a really interesting part of his personal brand. I won't share his secrets as to why, but it is safe to say that few others utilize that particular candy the way he does. And the fact that I was so excited about it sealed the deal that day. Kindred spirits bonding over atomic fireballs—what a hoot!

It was just after that when I asked Curt if I could attend his weekly meetings—in Cedar Falls. His requirement that I either "attend once and never again, *or* come every week" did not deter me. I showed up the next Monday—the only female in the room. Curt introduced me but did not otherwise offer a lot of information about me. One of the guys I remembered from college, though I didn't know him personally. He was a star basketball player named Randy Kraayenbrink—his name was too long for the jersey, so they shortened it to K'brink. Every time he made a basket, the crowd would roar, "K'brink!" But other than that, I had no connection to any of these guys.

At a certain point, Todd, another guy in that office, leaned back in his chair. It made a loud crack, and he bent over to see what had happened. He picked up a piece of the chair from the floor, and Randy smirked and said, "Looks like you lost your nut."

It was one of those turning points—a test, if you will. Everyone held their breath—they wanted to laugh, but weren't sure it was appropriate in "mixed company." What I did next would determine whether my presence would be welcomed or rejected. So I rolled my eyes, and with an exaggerated sigh said, "So *happy* to be here."

Everyone burst out laughing, and one guy said, "You're going to fit right in." I could have been offended and sternly reprimanded them in my best lawyer voice. But *why?* I thought it was a hilarious play on words. It wasn't threatening, it wasn't designed to be exclusionary or harassing. It was simply *funny.* And my willingness to go along with the joke allowed them to relax around me.

I attended every meeting after that, no matter the weather. And Highway 20 in the winter can be brutal. If the weather was bad, I would drive up the day before and stay with my friend Tracy. In fact, there was one month where I was there so often that on the first weekend I *wasn't* there, her husband looked around and asked where I was!

Why did I drive two hours up and two hours back for a meeting that lasted two hours plus lunch, sometimes in terrible weather? Because I had committed to it. Because it was important to me. And because there was incredible value in it. When I first started attending, I was in so far over my head, I couldn't even understand what they were talking about. I would leave with my head spinning, wondering what I had gotten myself into. But gradually I got to the point where I could understand what they were talking about. I couldn't *do* it yet, or even *teach* it to my clients yet, but I could at least understand it.

And then finally came the light bulb day—the day I *got it*. I understood it, I could do it, and I could contribute to the conversation. And I knew I had arrived when, in a meeting in Des Moines, a more veteran advisor asked me, "How do you know that?" My response (in my head) was, "How do you *not* know that, given how long you've been here?"

I am a person who gives credit where credit is due, but singing Curt's praises did occasionally create some challenges. I remember when Bob, a man in the Des Moines office, asked me if I would record Curt's meetings so he could learn as well (without the effort of the drive, of course). I passed the buck and told him I would ask Curt, but that it was his decision, not mine. Curt said no, for a number of very good reasons—which is exactly what I knew his answer would be. And then Bob said, "Well, I didn't think you would just ask him like that."

"Really?" I asked, puzzled. "What did you think I would do?"

"I thought you would just record it and let me listen to it." In other words, surreptitiously. I looked at him directly, rocked back on my heals and with a small smile, said, "Well! That would be dishonest." I don't think he quite got my pointed statement, but I was a bit more careful about "talking up" my experiences working with Curt to my Des Moines colleagues.

All of these experiences, as well as the many others I've not talked about, created quite a bond of loyalty. I tried to always give him credit where due, and I didn't allow people to unfairly criticize him—even the boss. When he would tell me to do something differently from how Curt taught me, I would politely explain why I was doing it that way. If I couldn't get him to agree, I simply told him I would "consider" it and then ignore him.

I trusted Curt's judgment because I felt like Curt's focus was on helping people and improving their financial lives. It wasn't about him—it was about the clients. That lined up with my own values, so I did what *he* told me—not the boss. I owed Curt a *lot*. So when I decided to leave the financial industry, I felt a tremendous amount of guilt, but I had to tell him my decision.

We had lunch at the Other Place when he was in Des Moines, and I told him I had put in my notice. He looked surprised and then said with great sincerity, "I'll miss you!" I laughed and said, "Oh, no. I'm not quitting *you*—just the company and the industry. I still need your help and your mentoring." He listened quietly as I told him about my prayer years before for a *life* mentor, rather than just a professional mentor. I shared Susan's observation that perhaps his role in my life wasn't limited to being a professional mentor, which reminded me of that long ago prayer. And I concluded by telling him, "God definitely over-blessed me when He answered that prayer."

We spoke a bit about what I was going to be doing—writing and speaking. He cautioned me to not forget about the marketing piece. Although it would be easier to talk to businesses about what I was doing (as opposed to asking friends and family to come talk to me about their money), and it would be about something I was more passionate about, the prospecting would still be a challenge for me.

Although there were a few wins after that conversation, they were few and far between. Now it was 2014, and I had been out on my own for over a year. Curt and I were having lunch again, this time at Chick-Fil-A (I *love* that place!). I was being gently scolded for my sales call "reluctance." Our conversations tend to jump around, and that day, I had also talked to him about the concept of developing a personal board of directors, as well as a meeting I had had earlier in the day with a prominent businessman. Curt tied all those topics together with one simple question: "Did you ask him to serve on your board?"

"No," I confessed. "I have trouble asking." After a beat, I looked him square in the eye and asked, "Would *you* serve on my board?"

It's rare for Curt to simply agree to something like that, at least with me. Typically, he throws in some good-for-me conditions, and this time was no exception. He agreed on the condition I had to have at least four or five people on the board—he didn't want to be a board of one. When I agreed, he sat back and said, "See? You *can* ask." I responded that it took a lot of courage to ask him. He shrugged and said, "So be courageous." Ah, so easy for him, so difficult for me.

Now, a personal board of directors works differently from a professional one in two significant ways. First, you don't typically meet with the full board, and second, the member's advice isn't limited to work-related issues. There were four people on my board initially, and the structure worked well for the most part. But at a certain point, I was struggling a bit with Curt's role.

Being a writer and speaker are far different from being a financial advisor. And Curt's strengths with regard to sales and marketing are quite different from mine, which meant that the processes that worked for him didn't always work for me. Curt never sold anything, but people were lining up to buy from him. He cared deeply about his clients, and his focus was always on serving them. Yet he was never afraid of being perceived as imposing or being pushy—because he *wasn't* either of those things. He was just so confident that people needed what he had to offer that he wanted to share his knowledge with whomever God sent his way.

I, on the other hand, struggled. I'm an introvert, so the traditional ways of prospecting, such as networking events and cold/warm calling, were definitely not in my wheelhouse. Mingling was exhausting, and simply walking up to someone I didn't know was intimidating. And we all know what we do when faced with a task we don't like or we're not good at—we avoid it.

I began to feel stressed because I wasn't succeeding at doing things the way Curt did them, and I felt like I was constantly under threat of being "fired." Although I had always looked forward to our meetings and conversations, now I began to dread them, because I was failing.

In January 2015, we met early in the month rather than later, which was our usual schedule. I was excited about the things I was working on for the new year, but Curt seemed less so. He again made a vague reference to coming off the board at the end of the year. Although he couched it in terms of, "boards need to be refreshed," and, "I'm a starter—I like to get people going and then bow out," all I *heard* was, "You're failing, and I'm not going to continue to waste my time with you." It was brutal, and I could barely hold back the tears.

In the time between that meeting and the next one, in late February, I made a radical decision. I would *not* focus any attention on prospecting for new consulting clients. I would focus nearly all my attention on writing. Prospecting had become a mental distraction that was keeping me from writing, which was the very thing I had left the financial job to do. But I wasn't doing much of it other than blog posts because I was so stressed out about trying to succeed at *prospecting*.

As the time for my February meeting with Curt drew nearer, I became increasingly agitated. Although I knew I had done a *lot* in the two months since we last spoke, I didn't know whether Curt would see it that way. Would this be the month he "resigned"?

The night before Curt and I were to talk, I prayed about it. Quietly, the answer began to reveal itself—I needed to let him go as a board member. I didn't even recognize it initially; my resistance saw it first and tried to hide it from me. I didn't *want* to let him go as my mentor and board member. I love the conversations I have with him, because of three things: Content, pace and philosophy—those three things line up just right to create great conversations. We talk about big ideas, he moves quickly through the conversation because he doesn't have to "wait" for me to catch up, and we share many values and philosophies.

I had grown tremendously under his mentoring and felt like I was just a better person overall.

And now I was being asked to release him? To give this up?

Yes. And even though I knew that was the right answer, I cried. I don't like it when people who are important to me leave my life. But what I realized was that *I* wasn't enjoying the relationship as it was now, and all signs indicated that he wasn't, either. However, that didn't necessarily mean I had to give up the friendship or the mentoring relationship we had—just the board member relationship. *That* is where things had gone awry. And, in fact, what I began to realize was that giving him up as a board member freed me from the pressure (he would probably use the word "accountability") to meet his "expectations" and simply learn from him. It would allow me to have conversations about the ideas and philosophies I valued so highly, without the stress of "disappointing" him.

Someone once observed that when she surrendered the things God asked her to surrender, they often came right back to her in an even bigger and more meaningful way. I realized I was trying to hold on to Curt as a board member because I thought that if he didn't have that official, *professional* role in my life, he wouldn't be in my life at all.

Good thing my theme this year is *Be Strong and Courageous,* because it was going to take a significant amount of courage to let go here.

I practiced what I would say, and when Curt called, I took a deep breath and began pacing (my *modis operandi* whenever I am on the phone, frankly). After the pleasantries, I began to explain what I had been thinking and praying about. I told him of my tendencies to hold on to things (and people) too long. Curt has a deep wellspring of faith unmatched by anyone I know that is not clergy (and deeper than some of them as well, I suspect). He recognizes the importance of prayer and listening to God. Yet my decision to let him go seemed to catch him off guard a bit (which, as I've already noted, almost never happens with him).

We had a really great conversation, and in the end, I remained on his calendar. In other words, after I let go, he returned.

But that's not the end of the story. Our first meeting after this board "dissolution" was a face-to-face meeting over coffee, and the old camaraderie was back. We talked about books we were reading, work we were doing and our families (I've never met someone so devoted to his wife and committed to his marriage—it's truly inspiring). And we talked about my book. I told him that the working title was *Let it Go,* and that each essay was about something different I had to learn to let go of, whether it was a belief, a thing or a person. I told him that my idea for the cover was that of a young girl letting go of a bouquet of colorful balloons.

He looked thoughtful, and after a moment, asked about an alternative perspective—that of opening up. While he agreed that there were certainly things people needed to let go of, he was concerned that some might resist letting go—just like I do. They would pull it back and say, "That's fine for you, but you don't understand. My thing is different. I *can't* let it go." Letting go had a negative connotation, often associated with pain. But what if I looked at it as opening up to new possibilities, new perspectives and new opportunities?

And with that question, we were off to the races. We started talking about hands. When you are thirsty and hold your hands under water as a fist, you will not capture enough to quench your thirst. The water will simply bounce off. But if you open your hands, you can hold plenty of water. You won't hold all of it, but you will hold what you need.

Likewise, when we hold on tightly to *whatever* we're hanging on to in our lives, there is no room for new things to come in. But if you open yourself up to possibility, some things will stay—the things that *should* stay—and other things will naturally fall away, opening up space for new beliefs, new things and new people. When your hand is in a fist, there's only darkness inside. Opening your hands allows the light to come in.

Well, this was getting pretty deep. So of course, he flipped the conversation. With his usual quirky humor, he admitted that there were some things that needed to be let go of. "When the cat dies, you need to bury it," he observed. I burst out laughing. Initially, I thought this "analogy" would have applied to the nightmare of losing my house. But even there, had I been open to other possibilities rather than just "keep or let go," I could have had a different outcome.

Ultimately, Curt helped me see that there are some things that we don't need to aggressively "let go" of. We don't need to turn our hands upside down so that *everything* falls away. And although I didn't realize it at the time, that was the perfect description for what I had done with him. In my mind I thought I had "let him go" as a board member. But what had really happened was that I had opened myself up to the possibility of what the relationship might look like if I wasn't holding on to the *board* membership with a death grip. He didn't *come back*, as I thought; he never left. He just settled into a different role.

His insight also helped me realize why I was struggling with certain chapters in this book. I was viewing things as too black and white; things either stayed or they went. My editor had previously suggested that perhaps I needed a few more chapters about the positive aspects of letting go. But because I, by and large, equated "stay" with good and "letting go" with pain, I had difficulty seeing more than a handful of positive examples of letting go. But by adding a third, middle ground, it opened up (pun intended) a much more expansive—and positive—view of letting go.

Which is why the cover of the book now has hands open to receiving abundant water, keeping only that which is intended to stay, instead of a girl releasing balloons.

I might have to actually pay that guy for his ideas someday. Or maybe I'll just invite him to write a book with me.

CHAPTER 7
THE LITTLE THINGS

I t's the little things that undo me. Give me a full-blown crisis (like my husband's quintuple bypass surgery in 2008 and a broken back a few years later), and I can lock down my feelings and do what needs to be done efficiently and effectively. I am able to simply put one step in front of the other until I reach the other side. But if I am coming home, arms laden with my laptop, purse, grocery bag, and coffee *and* the door is locked when my husband is home—well, that's when I'm likely to have a meltdown.

It seems ridiculous when viewed from the perspective of a little more sleep and a little more time, yet I consistently fall into the same pattern. I find myself muttering things like, *REALLY? Why does everything have to be so DIFFICULT?!*

One day, while working in the financial industry, I shut my office door because I was afraid the newbie across the hall might become alarmed at all my muttering (that particular muttering was about forgetting to take the blue paper out of the printer and reload with white, necessitating not only reprinting, but a walk *all the way down the hall* to shred the blue paper—tragic, I know).

But I also notice that the little things tend to undo me when I am under more stress generally. It sometimes results in what I call "kick the dog" syndrome. You know—Dad has a bad day at work, so he comes home and yells at mom, who scolds the child, who kicks the dog. The dog, of course, is wondering, "*What the heck just happened? What did I do?*"

I found myself on the shameful end of this story when we moved into our condo after losing our house. I was physically exhausted from the move itself, of course, but also feeling mentally and emotionally "beat up" by the bank, its attorneys, and the court. So when the satellite TV guy gave me bad information, which led to an incorrect decision as to whether we stay with one company or switch to another (good grief—talk about a first-world kind of problem), I lost it. To his credit, he called me out on my bad behavior and said, "Why are you yelling at *me?*" (Technically, I wasn't *yelling,* but it was clear I was very angry.) I hung up. I had reached the end of my rope, and there was no knot to hang onto. I was done. I was kicking the dog.

After I calmed down, I texted him an apology, which he accepted, in spite of the fact that I didn't deserve it. Pure grace.

There's plenty of research out there to show that when we are under significant stress, we are less capable of coping with smaller stresses or making good decisions. And Lord knows I have been under significant stress. Yet, I'm not willing to let myself off the hook that easily. It's as though, because I'm in such pain, I want to punish those who are creating additional obstacles and difficulties in my life. As though they are *intentionally* trying to make my life difficult. I start seeing problems, and I, to quote my mother, make mountains out of molehills.

I have trouble letting go of the little things. I forget about grace.

People have shown me grace when I least deserved it (which is really the point of grace, after all). It's like that saying, "Be kind to everyone you meet, for everyone is fighting a battle you know nothing about." We don't know what battles others are facing. Mine nearly always tend to revolve around financial difficulties, but others are dealing with health issues, relationship issues or substance abuse. A parent is sick or dying; a child is struggling in school; their spouse is abusive; they've just lost their job. The list goes on and on. Yet I act as though I'm the only one in the world with problems.

But my own experiences *have* made me more empathetic, more compassionate and more understanding.

During the first open enrollment period after the Affordable Care Act (a/k/a Obamacare) was passed, my husband came home complaining about a man who was "rude" to the people conducting the meeting. I listened patiently, then shrugged and said, "Well, right—he's scared." Randy looked at me, confused, and said, "What?" I elaborated that because the guy had several children, the significant increase in his premiums scared him. He's worried about paying for it, about continuing to provide for his family. He's afraid of a situation that he has little control over, so he's "kicking the dog." Rather than berate him for being rude, someone needs to help him figure out a solution—and reduce his fear.

But if it's the little things that can cause the greatest challenges, it is also the little things that can make the biggest *positive* difference in my life.

Logan has a cat named Felix (and in a stunning display of age disparity, had no *idea* what I was talking about when I began singing, "*Felix, the cat, the wonderful, wonderful cat...*"). We think the cat is part mountain lion, given its size. It's already bigger than his girlfriend's dog, Willie, although to be fair, the dog is part dachshund, part Chihuahua (I'll give you a moment to picture *that*). Felix is all white except for a gray "Mohawk" that adds a needed bit of character and distinction. Felix is also a playful kitten, especially when Willie is around. They wrestle, chase each other up and down the hall and miss each other when the play date is over.

Logan lives in Denver, so normally I wouldn't get to experience all the awesomeness that is Felix, but because of a little app called

Snapchat, I can feel like I'm right there. Now, I know Snapchat is used for less savory pictures and videos, but given that my contacts are my kids, it's probably obvious that's not how *we're* using it.

Because Logan is in Colorado, he's an hour behind me in Iowa. And he works as a server, so often doesn't get home until well past *my* bedtime (especially since my bedtime is 9 p.m.—plenty of time for sleep before the 5:30 a.m. alarm goes off). This means that he often gets home from work and captures a quick video of Felix playfully raising havoc before Logan goes to bed.

Sometimes I'll wake up in the night, and because I don't have a clock by my bedside, I will check my phone to see what time it is. Whenever there is a notification that I have a new Snapchat from Logan, I smile. I don't watch it right then, of course, but I know it's waiting for me in the morning, starting me off with a smile at Felix's antics.

I get one of these almost daily, sometimes multiple times. I don't need to save them, although I did ask him to send a more permanent photo of him holding both animals, while teaching his girlfriend to play cribbage. I've entitled it "Card sharks." I use it as Logan's contact picture, and so whenever he calls, I laugh at the picture that comes up. It's a little thing, but it makes me smile.

Sometimes these little things come from complete strangers. My business cards are square ones from Moo.com. When I got my first order, I opened it up to see the first card, which was a bright teal, and said, "You're delightful." What a quirky, fun thing to see! I have it on my bulletin board, and it makes me smile whenever I look at it.

One of my daily habits is to be a blessing to someone. It doesn't have to be a big, Mother Teresa-sized blessing—anything that makes someone smile, makes their day a bit easier or is an unexpected courtesy qualifies. And sometimes these opportunities to bless show up in unexpected places, at unusual times. One such surprise occurred last October on my birthday.

Because Facebook "reminds" us of birthdays, people are inundated with good wishes (frankly, it's one of the best things about Facebook, if you ask me). Some people respond the next day with a group thank you, while others reply individually. I had decided to reply individually, but then for some reason, I decided to also say something positive about that person.

For some, it was a memory we shared. For others, it might be a small thing they did for me that meant a great deal. Still others were appreciated for their positive posts on Facebook—not the "shared" quotes, but loving, fun stories about family events, for example.

And some of the things that came back to me from that one little act of gratitude brought tears to my eyes. People opened up and shared their love for their spouse, their families and their faith. Others reciprocated the gratitude. They blessed me initially with their birthday wishes, I blessed them with gratitude, and they blessed me *again* with their response. I am hoping that this infinite loop of blessing also expanded to others in their lives. I know it made for a memorable day for me, and I plan to continue that tradition every year.

When I talked to Curt about the theme of *letting go,* he gave me a look and said, "But I don't want to let go of everything." As I wrote (okay, *re*wrote) this chapter, I realized that the small, everyday life events are an example of situations where you *don't* want to let go of everything—only the stuff that's not serving you. It's why the metaphor is of hands facing up, palms open. If your hands are clenched tightly in a fist, you can't let go of obstacles, nor can you receive new opportunities. If your palms are down, *everything* will fall out—the good *and* the bad.

But if your hands are open and facing up, the people and beliefs that should stay, will, while those that need to fall away will fall away. The micro-crises that drag me down and cause a meltdown will, if I let them, slip through my fingers, while the micro-blessings that daily bring joy to my life will rest easily in the palm of my hand, safely staying put.

If I let them, it's the little things that can tip my day toward gratitude and optimism.

CHAPTER 8

CONTROL

One of the hardest lessons I've had to learn is that I can't control everything in my life. I can plan to my heart's content, but far more often than I would like, there are unplanned deviations that take me down paths I would never have chosen.

Usually these involve my husband. And health "adventures."

I know I promised "in sickness and in health," but I didn't quite expect what was thrown our way. In 2008, Randy went in for his annual physical. Like any wife worth her salt, I had nagged him every year to go see the doctor. When he went this particular year, he told the doctor he was short of breath when he was shoveling snow. Because he had a history of high cholesterol *and* really bad family history, the doctor scheduled him for a treadmill test.

Randy came home and told me about the test, but he lied about why he was having it (which earned him my presence at every subsequent doctor's visit). His fiftieth birthday was approaching, so he told me it was just a precautionary, routine test because of his risk factors. He failed to mention the shortness of breath thing.

And then he flunked the treadmill test. So they scheduled an angiogram and said that if he needed stents, they would just do that at the same time. So he and I trekked down to Mercy Medical Center, which is where my cousin Gail works. They prepped him for the test and gave me a pager so I could go have lunch but still be reachable.

Gail and I went down to the McDonald's (why a hospital known for its cardiac care would have a *McDonald's* in its building is still a mystery to me). We hadn't been there long when she looked up and said, "Is that your pager?" There were so many beeps in McDonald's, I hadn't realized that one of them was the pager. She took me up the back stairs in record time (I had no idea where I was!), and was told that the procedure was over. This was a little concerning because of how fast it had been.

The doctor came in, along with a surgeon and a nurse. Randy was still groggy from his amnesia drug, but they told us that he had significant blockage and would need bypass surgery right away. They scheduled it for the following Wednesday (this was Friday), and then left so he could wake up.

The open-heart surgery lasted longer than it was supposed to. He received more plasma than anticipated. And instead of having quadruple bypass surgery, he ended up having quintuple (yes, *five*) bypass surgery. He was supposed to be in the hospital a total of three to five days, with one or two of those days in intensive care. Instead, he was in intensive care seven days and a regular room two days. Neither of us saw daylight for nine days.

There were of course, some light-hearted moments among the scarier ones. One of his nurses washed his hair with dry shampoo (that many days without a shower leads to a *really* bad case of bed-head), and told him she had added pink hair dye to it because he was causing her trouble (failing to use his spirometer, which probably led to some of his respiratory issues).

When he finally *did* get to take a shower, the hot water felt so good to him that he moaned in pleasure until I told him to stop or people would think he was doing something "inappropriate."

Then there was the day they removed his "Frankenstein" IV. It was in his neck and had multiple "ports." He thought we were kidding until he saw it (after the nurse obligingly dug it out of the trash).

Less light-hearted were some of the lessons he learned. For example, if someone told him to "take a deep breath," he knew it was going to hurt—a lot. When he coughed (to help keep his lungs clear), it was helpful to not only squeeze his red, heart-shaped pillow, but also to have someone hold and stabilize his ribs.

Returning home, he obviously had significant lifting restrictions. He slept in a recliner the first few nights because it was too uncomfortable laying flat in bed. I changed his dressings twice a day and made sure he was taking his meds (and he had a *lot* of meds when he came home from the hospital).

When he started going to the mall to walk, we would walk a short distance, and then he would sit down to rest. Because he struggled to get out of the chair, I had to pull him out—without pulling his stitches. And he couldn't drive, so I needed to drive him downtown for all of his cardiac rehab sessions.

Although clearly he had a tough go of it, those of you who are caregivers know that *that* job is no picnic, either.

But three years later, when he had his next health "adventure," that first caregiver experience looked like a piece of cake.

We were down at the lake with Jeff and Pam (Randy's older brother and his wife), and Randy decided he wanted to waterski. He had done a lot of skiing throughout his life, so it wasn't like he was trying to learn for the first time at age 53. And he had been fully cleared by his cardiologist, with no restrictions.

He tried to get up on the skis several times, and then on one particular fall—a rather innocuous looking one—he heard something pop and was in significant pain. Logan and my nephew, James, jumped in the water. Logan asked Randy if he could move his hands and feet, and he said, "Yes." The boys got him on the swim deck of the boat, and Jeff slowly motored back to the dock.

We got him out of the boat, *up the steep steps,* and into the house where he could lie down.

At a certain point, he said he wanted to go to the urgent care facility, which immediately told me he was really hurt. When we arrived, the waiting room was full. I got him a wheelchair, and we went in. We checked in but then had to wait. Randy was clearly uncomfortable, and finally said, "I'm going to pass out if I have to sit here much longer." So I went up to the counter, and they took him back to "triage" him again. It was then that I played the "heart surgery" card. Funny how quickly "he's going to pass out" and "quintuple bypass surgery" in the same sentence can get you a room.

Turns out he had broken his back.

It was a compression fracture (who knew that a 53-year-old male might have osteoporosis?), so sitting upright in that wheelchair while sitting in the waiting room was continuing to put pressure on the fractured vertebra. They transported him via ambulance (on a backboard and with a neck brace) to a university-affiliated hospital in a bigger city. They decided he did not need surgery, but he did need a "shell." This shell was custom made to fit him and had two hard plastic pieces: a front and a back, which reminded me of a turtle's shell and underbelly. These two pieces were connected by three straps on each side, each of which had to be drawn tightly so as to provide the correct amount of support. Despite the seriousness of the injury, he was discharged the next day, and I drove the remaining five-hour drive back to Des Moines, with him in the passenger seat, doped up on pain meds so he could make the trip.

But that was just the beginning.

For the first six weeks, he had to wear the shell 24/7—including while he was sleeping and showering. Six full weeks of pure discomfort on top of pain. And when he wasn't in the shower, he had to wear a T-shirt underneath the shell it so it didn't rub his skin raw. And one final requirement—under no circumstances was he to be vertical when the shell was off.

The morning routine, then, went like this: While he was still in bed, I would remove the shell and the T-shirt. Then I would put the shell back on him. Because he couldn't be vertical, this required a lot of rolling from side to side on his part. I wasn't strong enough to do all that from the side, so I had to straddle him (obviously not sitting *on* him and his broken back) to get enough leverage to pull the straps tight.

And it was much more difficult than it sounds. Once the shell was back on, he could get up and take his shower. After the shower, he had to lie back down on the now towel-covered bed. I took the shell off, dried him off (because he couldn't bend over with the shell on to dry off his legs, and he couldn't dry off his torso while lying in bed), and then put a clean T-shirt on, and *then* put the shell back on. It was physically exhausting for both of us. After the six-week mark, he could shower and sleep without wearing the shell, but had to wear it all other times. Even that small concession made a huge difference to him, and it eliminated a couple of the on-again, off-again steps for me.

I don't tell these stories so that you will feel sorry for him or for me. I tell them because neither the heart surgery nor the broken back was in my plan for how life would go.

And I am a planner. I get frustrated when there is no plan, and I get frustrated when things don't go according to plan. I do not like uncertainty and will tell anyone who will listen that chaos is not my friend. I don't like it when I can't control the outcome, which is another reason why losing the house was so unbearable. I couldn't control what the bank would agree to, and I couldn't control what the judge decided. I could do my part, and I could be as persuasive as I wanted, but ultimately I was forced to abide by their decisions. And to this day, I believe those were *wrong* decisions, both morally and legally. But I finally had to let it go.

Of course, health and financial adventures are not the only things that don't go according to plan.

I applied for a part-time administrative assistant job at my church, reporting to Shari, an associate pastor. This was a job I could have done with one hand tied behind my back. My first job out of college was that of administrative assistant to Samuel Levey, who was the Gerhard Hartman Professor and Head of the Graduate Program in Hospital and Health Administration at The University of Iowa (whew!). Additionally, Dr. Levey was the head of the search committee for the second-in-command position at The University of Iowa Hospitals and Clinics (one of the few tertiary level hospitals in the nation, at least at that time), *and* the editor of the professional journal, *The Journal of Hospital & Health Administration*. Although I was only 22 years old, Dr. Levey, a gruff perfectionist who spoke his mind whether you liked it or not, said that I was the best secretary he had ever had. I set up systems, taught myself word-processing and was efficient and cheerful.

So, no—a part-time administrative position at church was not going to be too difficult.

In addition to my regular resume, I sent a "church" resume. This outlined everything I have ever done at church and included such diverse roles as accompanying and playing for services, board positions and teaching Sunday School.

Although some questioned whether this position was beneath my education and experience, I wanted it because it would allow me plenty of free time to write while still bringing in some income. It was a job that would be easy for me, so I could save my mental energy for writing. And I could do a great job for the pastor I would report to. In short, it was perfect for me, and I was perfect for the job.

And I didn't get it.

Not because I wasn't qualified, or even *as* qualified as Alyssa, the person the pastor ultimately hired. No, I didn't get hired because I was a *member* of the church. Let that sink in for a minute. Shari explained that her research indicated that it was "cleaner" to hire a non-member, but while I understand the thinking behind it, I had two main problems with this concept. First, I noted that it was interesting that the church was willing to let me "work" for free week after week as a Deacon and choir accompanist, but when considering pay, wanted a non-member. And my parting comment was to say that I hoped Alyssa didn't want to join the church, because she would have to either quit or be told she *couldn't* be a member. The look on Shari's face told me she had not considered that possibility.

Shari and I met the following week, because I wanted her to understand how I felt about her decision (genuinely and logically, not in a mean or spiteful way). But ultimately, I told her that I would get over it, and the world wouldn't spin off its axis just because she didn't hire me. And again—although I think she made the wrong decision, it doesn't change the decision. And now *I* have a decision to make: I can sit in a corner and whine about how things didn't go according to (my) plan, or I can pick myself up, dust myself off, and let it go. Move on.

None of this means, of course, that I shouldn't plan or set goals. It does not mean I shouldn't take responsibility for my actions, or just sit around and see what happens. This leads to drifting, which is a dangerous way to live a life. But for me, it means that I need to let go of my propensity to rail against life when it doesn't go my way. My temper tantrums don't change anything, and they waste valuable energy that could be directed in more productive ways.

I don't always get what I want—none of us do. Things don't always go according to plan. Life surprises me—sometimes in wonderful ways, and sometimes in ways that are painful. But hanging on to what I believe *should* have happened isn't helpful. Yes, it's probably healthy to throw a pity party—a short one—and get it out of my system. But then I have to let it go, and instead of dealing with what I think should have happened, deal with what *did* happen.

CHAPTER 9

WHO DECIDES WHAT'S POSSIBLE?

When I was a student in Mrs. John's third-grade classroom, our high school boys' basketball team qualified for the state tournament. Since there was no such thing as Common Core back then, teachers were allowed to give *creative* assignments that encouraged *creative* thinking and writing. Mrs. John asked us to imagine what it would be like to be the basketball at the tournament, and to write from that perspective. My story went thus:

Being a Basketball

Help, here I am in Veterans Auditorium. This is the last place a basketball would want to be! These basketball players are so rough! They bounce you on the hard cold floor and then they toss you all over the place! You never know where you are going to be! And, OUCH, oh my, that smarts, then you are...OUCH... tossed up through the...OUCH...basket! Yow! I should have listened to my mother and OUCH become a doctor's bag! Oh! Youch! I'm going to...OUCH...End this story. YOUCH!

I also wrote a nonsense rhyme about a raccoon in a saloon that my teacher kept, but I will let you mentally write that one up with your own (third-grade) imagination.

How do I know this is what I wrote? Did my parents save it as a testament to my literary prowess, framed for the refrigerator gallery? No. My *teacher* saved it. I didn't remember anything about it until I visited her classroom *twelve years later*. I couldn't believe she had kept something I had written all those years ago!

Some twenty years after *that,* I sent her a letter telling her of the impact she had made in my life, which made us *both* cry when she called to thank me for the letter. She responded by sending me a copy of the story and the poem she had typed up for her file.

"Why did you keep these things all these years?" I asked her, truly amazed.

"Because they were really good," she answered.

The story had emotion, action and an unexpected twist at the end (the reference to the doctor's bag, in case that didn't jump out at you the first time). The overuse of exclamation points aside, it was an entertaining story to read.

Now, it's true that Mrs. John was a powerful influence in my life. It's also true that she made me feel smart and important, and that she let me stay inside for recess (yes, *let*—I hated going outside for recess, preferring instead to stay inside and read!). But knowing that she kept those third-grade writing samples because they were well written has had a powerful impact on my adult life as well.

When we are children, we naturally gravitate to the things we enjoy. We don't worry about whether they will pay well, whether they are too "silly" or whether we should perhaps instead do what "everyone else" is doing. We do them for the sheer pleasure they give us. We use our gifts, and we make our world joyful and childishly (in a positive way) productive.

And then we grow up.

We start listening to other people tell us what we can do, what we should do and, more devastatingly, what we cannot (or should not) do. We start being Responsible, not realizing that we have a responsibility to ourselves and our own gifts that far outweighs any responsibility to conformity and making others happy with our choices.

We get to the point where we no longer remember what makes us feel alive in our work; we can no longer identify our gifts. We can tell you what our experiences have been (educational and professional), we can tell you our competencies and point to "progressively increased supervision" responsibilities, but we can no longer tell you what we love to do. Or if we can, it's said with a wistful sigh, as though acknowledging the "reality" that we will never be able to do those things.

What are we *thinking*?

I floundered for many years trying to figure out what I wanted to do "when I grew up." I began explaining my resume diversity by saying I had a "portfolio career." I tried new things, but they were usually influenced by what other people wanted for me, had done themselves, or wanted me to do that would help *them*. Although I was better at some of these things than others, there were really none of them that I flat out *couldn't* do.

But I never truly loved any of them.

I read books like *What Color Is Your Parachute?* I took assessments, interviewed people about *their* jobs and went back to school. I prayed for guidance, asked for advice and tried my hand at a number of different things.

Nothing.

When a friend asked me what I wanted to do, I surprised myself by saying, "I want to write." His response?

"You can't make any money writing." And just like that, the dream was stomped out of existence.

I went back to the books, the assessments and the conversations, searching desperately for something *other than* what I really wanted. None of it seemed to help. Many books designed to help you find your best work ask questions like this one: *What is the one thing you love doing so much, you would do it for free?* Or, *What is the one thing that, when you are doing it, time just seems to fly—you're in the "flow?"* The problem is, there are many things I can do, so choosing just one is difficult. How do I know which one is the *right* one? And for free? We have bills to pay, remember? And regarding "flow"—I often feel it when I'm playing the piano, but I am not interested in pursuing a career as a pianist. Accompanying two children's choirs at church, with the occasional special event thrown in, are plenty for me right now.

But then I read a book that asked a different question—*What can you not stop doing?*

And once again, writing floated gently but a bit more insistently this time to the surface. As I thought about it in the context of the grammatically incorrect double negative, I realized that I couldn't stop writing. No matter what my job title was, I found a way to focus on writing. Whether I was writing a legal brief, a non-profit newsletter or a script for a style show introducing a new dress code, I *loved* writing. Who didn't? (Well—lots of people, as it turns out.)

Writing came effortlessly to me. It was a way for my introverted self to examine and then explain what I was thinking. When I wrote guest posts or articles, whether for print or online publications, there were few changes during the editing process. People told me they really enjoyed what I wrote, even if they didn't agree with it.

That break-through question didn't ask me to speculate on what I *might* like to do—it focused on what I was *already* doing. It helped me see the things that I was consistently, if subconsciously, gravitating toward. It identified the things that I most loved to do in *any* job, and how I had naturally expanded the opportunities to write, sometimes in unusual ways (like the style show).

And I realized why it meant so much to me to learn that Mrs. John had kept my writing. Yes, it was flattering, but it also reminded me of the gift I loved when I was a child. Her comments encouraged me to recapture the joy of expressing myself through the written word. She helped me remember who I was and what I had to contribute to this world.

I'm also pretty clear about what I write and don't write. I don't write fiction (other than when I was in third grade), and I don't write mysteries or poetry or romance. Could I? Maybe. But that's not the kind of writing I'm passionate about. I write non-fiction books and posts that are designed to help people, or to get them to *think* about things. Things that matter to me, like politics and education, personal growth, women's issues and faith.

Of course, this leads me to write things that occasionally get me into hot water. When I answered the provocative question about what I couldn't stop doing and decided to leave the financial industry, I just knew I wanted to make my way in the world as a writer.

I began writing two blog posts a week. There were some who suggested that I if I just wrote enough blog posts, I could turn those into a book. But I remembered an experience I once had, of buying a book written by a blogger whose work I enjoyed. The problem? The book was a collection of his posts, which meant that I had just paid $17 for a book full of things I had already read—for free. I vowed I would not do that to people. Besides, my posts were wildly varied in topic. The only thing they had in common was that they were things that just happened to catch my eye and provoke my thinking.

Voicing my opinions on Facebook and in blog posts caused a high school acquaintance to write a profanity-laced diatribe on my Facebook timeline, simply because I suggested that her use of the word "retard" was hurtful to some of our classmates who have children with Downs Syndrome (although I did *not* tell her she couldn't use the word). After leaving her comments up long enough to be entertained by friends and family who came to my defense, I unfriended *and* blocked her. I've been verbally attacked on Twitter for things I've said. My faith has been mocked, my positions argued with, and snide comments made. Despite being an attorney, I do *not* have particularly thick skin, and these things hurt me—deeply, sometimes.

But even though the "haters gonna hate," I can't *not* write. And with regard to my faith and political beliefs, I refuse to be silenced. I'm never rude, I don't call people names and I don't insist they agree with me. I simply ask questions and try to get people to see that there are different ways of looking at and thinking about things. As such, there is no reason for them to be rude and hateful to me—but that doesn't always stop them.

Some people, thankfully, are big enough to seriously consider what I have to say without getting defensive, and humble enough to find out if it's really true. Chris Conetzkey, editor of *The Des Moines Business Record*, met with me and wrote an editorial about our meeting after I took the *Business Record* to task over the lack of women on their list of Top 25 Business Leaders in Des Moines—there were *three*.

After our meeting, Chris went back to his office and began digging to see if what I had said about the underlying issues was true, and he wrote about not only that, but about steps they were taking to remedy the situation. When his story came out, my friend Michelle told me I was a "one-woman army," which I found funny. I hadn't set out to do anything big—I had merely written a comment on Facebook in response to something I thought was wrong.

In pursuit of my writing, the first year after I left the financial world, I joined a group that billed itself as a success club. As part of that, we were to choose a big, bold goal to pursue for that year. I chose writing a book as my goal. Yet despite the monthly check-ins, I couldn't seem to get it written. And the book itself bored me, so I abandoned it. But the thought of quitting altogether never seriously crossed my mind.

In the meantime, I was still trying to prospect and drum up business for my speaking. Prospecting is *not* a gift of mine, so it requires considerable effort, especially when I try to use methods that work for other people—people who have different strengths and personalities. During one of my quiet prayer times, I wearily asked God to tell me whom I should contact. I had made lists, I had tried to figure out who my "ideal client" was, and I had even had a few meetings. But nothing happens fast in the corporate world, and patience is not *my* virtue.

I was constantly trying to find new people to talk to while waiting for the ones I had met with to make a decision. I was tired of trying to find the next person or business that might be willing to meet with me, so I prayed desperately, "Just tell me who to contact, and I will make the call." Because God *loves* those kinds of prayers, right? The ones full of resignation and misery that ask Him to fix something we don't really want fixed, because it will then require us to do something we don't really want to do.

God in His wisdom did not give me any names. No holy paper airplanes gently descending with the "chosen ones" on a list. Instead, He gave me the question I wrote about in the Introduction.

"What if you gave yourself permission to simply *write* for the next 12 weeks?"

My eyes flew open, and I literally gasped out loud. My first thought was, "Is that *allowed? No prospecting?!*"

But I sat with the question for a while, turning it over in my mind to see if that was a viable option. What if I *could* just write for 12 weeks? As I allowed myself to seriously consider it as an option, a feeling of pure relief began to wash over me, and then excitement. But then doubt crept in. I had set the "big, bold goal" of writing a book in the past—without success. Why would this time be different? And if I couldn't get it done in 12 months, what made me think I could get it done in 12 *weeks?*

For once, though, I was able to reframe those questions. Instead of allowing them to overwhelm me and cause me to quit, I turned them into legitimate questions *that had an answer.* How *could* I make this time different? Why *had* I failed in the past to get the book done, despite the monthly accountability?

It's funny how answers and resources come to you just when you need them when you are on the right path. Shortly after asking that question, I came across a blog post that talked about goal setting. Since this was the beginning of the year, there was nothing surprising about that—the web is teeming with those kinds of posts. But this one was different.

This one suggested that the best way to reach your goals was to stop obsessing over them. I frowned. *What?* That seemed to contradict everything I had ever read about goal setting (and I had read a *lot*). I read further and experienced what Oprah calls an "ah-ha moment." What the writer was advising turned out to be one of those breakthrough strategies that immediately created positive results in my life.

What was his advice? Focus on the process, not the goal. Curt had been talking about process for years, but I never really *got it* until I read this post. When Curt talked about it, I thought of it as a glorified task list. That's not what he meant, of course, but that's what I heard. Viewing process as a to-do list cheapens its real power—the power to virtually guarantee success if you choose the right process and follow through with that process.

When I work with my coaching clients, I ask it this way: "What one *habit* (i.e., process) can you develop that will *inevitably* lead to your success?" For me, the habit of writing 2,000 words every day would inevitably lead me to my goal. In other words, if I wrote 2,000 words every day, I couldn't *not* have a book (whether it was a *good* book was another question, but I would have *a* book). And then when I did the math, I realized it would be done mid- to late February. The problem with my previous big, bold, *annual* goal of writing a book was that it was too much time. When I felt like I had "all the time in the world" to get it done, I procrastinated. There was no sense of urgency.

But to give my writing this intense focus also meant I wasn't going to have a lot of meetings or schedule a lot of time for prospecting. Meetings are the lifeblood of a financial advisor, but they kill writing, because as a writer, the time you spend *writing* is your lifeblood—not meetings. It was no wonder I was failing—I was trying to apply a process suited for one industry to a profession for which it was not suited at all. In doing so, I wasn't doing either thing well.

That laser focus, without the time and emotional distraction of prospecting, allowed me to write easily. In my head, I was shooting for an 80,000-word book. Google told me that was how many words an "average" book contained, but then I read a post by an author who was talking about *his* new book. It was his "longest book ever" and was 70,000 words. 70,000? That was his *longest* book? It occurred to me that Google might be wrong (who knew?), and that I should perhaps revise my expectation of length. Right on the heels of *that* revelation was this one: *I was going to be finished SOON.* Which meant, I needed to start thinking about finding an editor and make some decisions about publishing.

Previously, my strategic self would have tried to map out every detail of the book, from concept to writing to publishing to selling. But this time, I was trying to take it a step at a time, trusting that what I needed to know would show up when I needed to know it. My first and primary purpose was to simply *write* the book. But now that it was close to finished, it *was* time to think about next steps. And within two weeks I talked to no less than five different people about that. Money showed up to make editing and self-publishing through Amazon Create Space possible. No more than I needed, and no less.

The editing and revising process is going well (except for Chapter 2, which is kicking my proverbial keister, and which I will probably leave out altogether), and is even ahead of schedule. It feels like being a child again and doing something for the sheer joy of it: following *my* gifts, not others' expectations.

Betty White, the brilliant comedienne, was recently asked if she had any regrets. She noted that she wished she had said yes to her husband's marriage proposal earlier. If she had, they would have had another full year together, rather than wasting that time by being apart. I feel the same about my writing. I regret listening to other people tell me I couldn't make money at it (although it's entirely possible they may yet turn out to be right), letting other people decide what I should do and be. The good news is, when I finally opened up to the possibility that *I* might know better than "other people" what my gifts were and how they ought to be used, things started moving. Ideas flowed, and a book has been written.

Hold tightly to your dreams, and let go of other people's expectations of how you should use your gifts. *You* get to make that decision. *Trust yourself.*

CHAPTER 10

THE OPEN DOOR

By now, you've perhaps guessed that I am a voracious reader. I love connecting ideas from different writers and genres. Books help me make sense of my world and the people in it. Part of my love of reading is, logically enough, because I'm a writer. But I've always loved books. When I was in the fifth grade, I had the best "job" ever—I got to help the school librarian.

This was before digital checkouts, of course, so I would help put the pockets in the books for the cards you signed when you checked out a book. I loved stamping the due date on the cards and re-carding and re-shelving the books that were returned. And if it was a really good day, I might even get to *type* the labels that went on the back of the spine!

I usually arrived at school about a half hour before school started, and Mrs. Morse (who called all us kids "honey") let me hang out with her in the library in the mornings before school, before the library was even open. It was a haven for me, and I loved spending time there. It was safe, it was comforting, and it was *quiet*. But sometimes safe and comfortable is not where we need to be.

Someone who knows my love of reading just sent me John Ortberg's book, *All the Places to Go: How Will You Know?* And yes, it does reference the Dr. Seuss book by a similar name, but with a little different spin. Although it is a faith-based book, the basic premise has an equally secular application about decision-making. Doors will open all the time; the question is—will you step through them?

My habit, unfortunately, is to look at the door and wonder who opened it (God or the "other party"), what's on the other side, *which* door is the right one and, finally, as if all that isn't exhausting enough, whether the door is opening, or whether I am breaking it down to chase a dream that isn't meant for me.

I don't remember this paralyzing analysis in my earlier years. In high school, I chose jobs I thought sounded fun. I did things because I simply *wanted* to—no justification required. I hung out with good people and willingly left behind those relationships that were not healthy. My eyes were clearer, then, unclouded by what others might think, or the consequences of making a "wrong" decision in situations that really had no clearly wrong decision. But somewhere along the line, I lost that.

Oddly enough, despite my desire to control and plan everything to within an inch of its life, *not* being the decision-maker can sometimes make me braver and less concerned about the outcome. This only works if I trust the person who *is* the decision-maker, however. Because responsibility for the outcome lies further up the food chain, I can simply relax and do my part.

Learning to let go of this insistence to always know how something will turn out is difficult for me, but the times I have relinquished control over the outcome have inevitably been the times I've been more successful, probably because there's less pressure to get it *right*. Right can simply happen, instead of being chased down and forced into submission.

When I was in college, this showed up in a general education class I took called (I kid you not) *Culture of the Ghetto*. It was taught by an African-American professor and was a popular class on campus. As you might imagine with a title like that, we had rather unusual "textbooks," such as the classic book *Think and Grow Rich,* along with unique, *illuminating* field trips with lots of "ah-ha" moments.

One such experience required that we attend a black-owned restaurant that was trying to succeed in the "ghetto" of Waterloo, Iowa. I sat down at the counter next to a couple of my classmates. The woman behind the counter had a scar that ran from her ear downward, disappearing into her dress. We did *not* ask how she got it, but I'm pretty sure it wasn't open-heart surgery (my husband has those scars, and they look nothing like hers).

She snapped her towel over her shoulder in a practiced, habitual way, put her hand on her hip and asked what we wanted. The girl next to me, clearly terrified by this intimidating woman, squeaked out an order for an English muffin. The woman behind the counter pursed her lips and then said, with epic disgust, "We got *toast.*" The unspoken *Duh* was clearly heard. My classmate's eyes opened wide, and she hurriedly said, "Toast is good. I'll have that." Talk about letting go of a comfort zone!

We also had an unusual "semester project." We were to pick something we wanted—a goal—and visualize the achievement of that goal. We were to spend 30 minutes every day for 21 days thinking about it. We were *not* to worry about whether it was possible or how we might attain (or obtain) the object of our heart's desire.

Normally, of course, the strategist in me would have insisted on being able to plan it all out before committing to *anything,* even visualizing. But because this was a homework assignment and I was specifically instructed to *not* worry about how it might happen, I simply did the assignment. We weren't graded on whether we actually *achieved* the goal, just whether we followed the process. So I did it. The fact that I wasn't obsessed with the assignment turning out a particular way freed me of the pressure to *make it* happen. It allowed me to focus on the process. And because it was a homework assignment and not "real world," I didn't overthink whether it was the "right" goal. I simply chose something I wanted and did the visualization. What did I choose, you ask?

My own apartment.

Now, I was a full-time college student working as a part-time grocery clerk. I wasn't a trust fund baby and wasn't anticipating any long-lost relative dying and leaving me a boatload of money with no grief strings attached. But it was one of the greatest examples of not needing to see the whole staircase before taking the first step that I have ever successfully pulled off. If I had tried to plan that one out, I would have given up before I started. I would not have been able to figure out how to "make" it happen; financially, it was too far beyond comprehension to be realistic.

But since I wasn't being graded on whether I actually *achieved* the goal, I wasn't limited in what I chose. I simply chose what I really wanted. I dutifully sat still every day, quietly visualizing my goal (being an introvert was a definite plus here). I thought about what it would look like, the music I might play in my apartment (probably Huey Lewis and the News at that time), the tastes of the food I would cook (or order in—probably pizza), the smell of candles.

I visualized myself studying in my apartment, leaving for work in the afternoon and returning home late at night, and the giddy feeling I would have knowing that the space was *all mine*. I wasn't going to be awakened at 3 a.m. when roommates came home from the bars and kicked popcorn bowls (that I may or may not have been guilty of leaving on the dorm room floor). I wouldn't be frustrated when a roommate left a mess in the kitchen or had her stuff all over the bathroom. And I wouldn't worry about any unknown "guests" that might be sleeping on my couch.

And guess what? Before the end of the semester, I did, in fact, move into my own apartment. If I had insisted on figuring out how to "make" it happen, though, I would never have succeeded, because it came about in a very unusual way—one I could not have planned.

As I got older, though, I made mistakes—sometimes costly mistakes—which caused me to be hesitant about other decisions. I didn't trust myself as much anymore, and I lost a big part of myself in this quest to be an adult. I stopped walking through doors, confidently assuming that everything would work out, knowing too well that things often did *not* work out well.

I often find myself standing on the threshold of the open door, craning my neck trying to see all the way down the "hallway." The door begins to close, which restricts my view even more, until it finally closes. And then I simply say, "Well, I guess that wasn't the right door for me." But doors don't stay open forever, and the closing of a door doesn't necessarily mean it wasn't right for me. It means I didn't step through it while it was open.

I missed out on a job once because it happened too fast, if you can believe that. A recruiter friend of mine recommended me for a position. In the space of two weeks, I interviewed, spent two *paid* days job shadowing, and was ultimately offered the position. And I turned it down. I had my reasons at the time (remember my penchant for wanting to have *reasons,* so I'm not to blame?). But in retrospect, I think it just happened too fast. I didn't have time to *think* about whether it was the right decision and didn't have the courage or the confidence to just jump in and see what happened. That's just not how I'm wired, unfortunately. And there was no one in my life at that time to encourage me to just do it.

I want to let go of the need to manage and plan everything, and to know exactly how every last little thing is going to turn out. I want to let go of being so *serious* about my life. I want to have fun, both in my work and play. I want to trust myself again.

And I want to walk through the doors God has opened for me and see what's on the other side, confident in the knowledge that even the wrong door can be made right if walked through with the right heart.

CHAPTER 11

MY DAD

When I was 12 years old, my dad died. This was not a voluntary letting go. This was a kicking and screaming (literally), ripping-him-from-my-life theft.

Even writing that sentence causes me to become very, very still, so that the sorrow doesn't overwhelm me. It's been nearly *40 years* since that horrific day, yet I still cry when I think of it. The memory is scorched into my brain, such that even if I should be stricken with dementia late in life, I feel I will remember *that* event.

My parents had been married for fourteen years before I was born. They had been told they would never have children, so my appearance was a joyful surprise—or, as the doctor called it, a "fluke." Three years later, there was another "fluke" in the form of my brother.

My Aunt Mickey tells a story about the first time she met me. I was napping, but Dad went right in and picked me up to show me off to her. She told him that it was clear he was going to need some new shirts—the buttons were just *popping off* the one he was wearing, he was so proud!

Because my parents had to wait so long for kids, they didn't want to waste a minute of that time, so they didn't often go out with friends. But on Monday nights, Dad bowled with the other men from church, and the wives went along and visited with each other. I could never sleep until they were home and I knew they were safe. This Monday night was no different. But Tuesday morning certainly was.

My grandmother was staying with us at the time, having just had surgery. This meant that she was sleeping in my brother's bed, while he slept on the couch. I remember being in that in-between state of consciousness between being asleep and awake, and hearing my nine-year-old brother start screaming. It felt muffled, like when you are under water. But I instinctively knew I did *not* want to wake up and hear what had happened.

When there was no other option but to wake up, I saw my minister, Reverend Henry, sitting by my bedside. My sense of dread increased. My mother broke the news to me, saying, "God wanted your dad." I was confused. *For what?* When it finally dawned on me that he had died, I felt like all the oxygen had been sucked out of the room. Nothing in my life had prepared me for something this devastating.

I think my parents probably knew that Dad was not going to live much longer, but they did not share that with us. While I understand they made that decision to protect us, it also deprived us of the opportunity to say good-bye, to prepare for and understand what was happening.

He had his first heart attack in April and was one of the early bypass surgery patients. At that time, children generally weren't allowed to visit people in the hospital, but they made an exception for us. We couldn't go to his room, though; he had to come to a lounge area. I seem to recall him walking in, rather than being in a wheelchair, although that could be wrong. I suspect that even if they wanted him to be in a wheelchair, he would have obstinately refused. He was in pajamas and a robe, which was a bit disconcerting because he wasn't really a pajama kind of guy. The strong man

I knew got up and got dressed; there was no lounging around in pajamas! He showed us the scar on his leg where they had pulled out the vein for the bypass, and told us he would be home soon.

And in January, just nine months later, he was gone.

Between his first heart attack and the final one, there was one hint of how ill he really was, although I completely missed it at the time (I was only 12, after all). I remember wandering into the living room one day. My dad was sitting in the recliner, and my mom in a chair opposite him, crying.

Now that, in and of itself, was of little concern—my mom cried at Hallmark commercials just as easily as *real* tear-inducing events. But the television wasn't on, so I asked my dad, "Why is Mom crying?" I think he tried to tell me, saying, "My heart isn't too strong." But even with that, I didn't get it, and I didn't ask any further questions. I knew his heart wasn't "strong"—he had had a heart attack. But that just didn't translate to him dying. I mean, really—whose dad dies when you're 12 years old? It was so far beyond anything I had ever experienced that it just didn't occur to me he might actually *die*.

At a certain point on the morning he died, I remember asking if I had to go to school. Although it sounds like a silly question, at the time it felt legitimate; in our house, you had to be pretty darn sick to miss school. When I was told no, I would be staying home, I pulled on the ugliest clothes I could find to signify the ugliness of the day—red polyester pants that were too short, and a shirt to match. And then I was lost. What did one *do*, when one's father had just died?

Although some details are vivid, others are a bit fuzzy. I had to call Mrs. Gilbert, my youth leader, because I was supposed to take dinner to youth group the next night. Unskilled as I was at breaking bad news, I simply blurted out, "I can't bring dinner tomorrow night. My dad died today." Poor Mrs. Gilbert! How do you respond to that?

But while I remember the call, I don't remember why *I* made it. When my kids were about the same age as me and my brother were when my dad died, it occurred to me that I *never* would have expected them to make a call like it if Randy had died. But I don't remember if my mom told me to call, or if I just did it without much discussion. That part of the memory is lost. Before I had kids, I didn't think about it much; it was just part of the story. Now I realize what an incredible thing it was to have a child make that call.

People stopped by, of course. My aunt and uncle from Michigan drove down to help. A man my father worked with on the loading dock of H&W Motor Express brought leftover cans of coffee—left over from what people brought *him* after his mother died the previous week. I remembered that dad and I had gone to the funeral home to pay our respects just two days prior. Every time someone stopped by, or I heard my mom tell someone that "Albert passed away," I ran into my bedroom, flung myself on the bed and cried my heart out.

The funeral was on Friday and was just as awful as you might expect. Many of my teachers were there. I was surprised to see them, and it seemed odd to think that my classmates had *lots* of substitute teachers that day because of me.

We rode to the gravesite in a gold limousine. I have *never* ridden in a stretch limousine since then. Not for proms or weddings or anything else. They symbolize death to me.

I never felt like I could let go of the grief. I hadn't fully or properly processed it when I was a child. Back then, there was no Amanda the Panda (a local Children's and Family Grief Center) to help kids and surviving parents deal with the emotions and even the practical aspects of grief. The prevailing thought was that kids were resilient. And they are, but it's easier to be resilient if you can appropriately process grief in the first place.

I couldn't talk to my mom about it, because every time I tried, she cried—and who wants to make their mom cry? So I just stopped asking. Which is unfortunate, because I don't feel like I have as many memories and stories about my dad as I should. I don't blame anyone for this. I believe everyone around me did the best they could in a very difficult situation.

I do have some memories, of course. I remember how he used to stand, hands on hips, rocking back and forth on his heels. I remember he used to call me Gina Marie, and the story behind my name. As I recall, Marie was a woman who had been kind to him and his fellow soldiers in Arizona, but who had been killed in a bicycle accident (although that, too, could be wrong—it's hard to remember that far back).

My parents liked the name Gina, but because my dad was always being mistaken for Italian (not that there's anything wrong with being Italian, of course. It's just that when you're *not* Italian and everybody keeps asking if you *are* Italian—well, it gets old), he was concerned that a name like Gina would *really* cause people to assume I was Italian. (I unfortunately got my mother's fair skin, however, so that might not have been as big a concern) I always wished they *had* named me Gina—it seemed much more glamorous than plain old Jean. So when he called me Gina Marie, it was a big deal.

I remember working on cars with him. My 95-year-old great-aunt stunned me once by telling me she thought I would grow up to be a mechanic! For someone in her generation to even consider that as a possible career for a woman was amazing. But when I asked her why she thought that, she said, "You always had your head under the hood of a car with your dad." It was true, but as I look back, I wonder if my dad was ever criticized for teaching me how to do things that were decidedly not "girly." My dad could fix anything, and he could build anything, and I like to think I got at least a little bit of that talent from him.

He built a trailer that we loaded up and took camping every August (we always went to ice-cold Clear Lake). He built an ingenious rack for hardware like screws, nuts and bolts that hung above his workbench. And he built me a "kitchen" complete with two cabinets, three drawers, a closet for my Susie Homemaker vacuum cleaner, and a countertop. I had a highchair (whose tray actually lifted up and down) and a crib. All built by him. (Maybe some girly things to offset the car mechanic image).

My extended family is, paradoxically, deeply faithful, yet also rather rough-and-tumble, never shying away from a fight. My dad said to me, "You are not to start a fight. But if someone else starts it, you need to be the one to finish it." My daughter thinks it's fantastic that he gave his *daughter* this advice. We were also expected to defend our family against "outsiders." You might be fighting with your sibling, but you had better defend that same sibling against others if necessary, or there would be heck to pay when you got home.

In a time when race issues were heating up, my father was unafraid to take his own siblings to task over certain language usage. This wasn't political correctness—this was an honest way of *being*. He explained that, although he knew that's how *they* were raised (like most of their generation), he did not want his own children raised that way. I think this was due in part to an experience he had as a young man.

My dad was a twin; there were ten children in his family, seven of whom were boys. When my Uncle Bill (who would later receive the Purple Heart for an injury he received on Iwo Jima) and Aunt Marthalee were living in Florida, there was a period of time when the family didn't hear from them. Grandma was getting worried, so my dad and his twin (Alfred) decided to drive down and see what was going on.

For whatever reason, they cut the top off the vehicle before they left. My dad tanned quickly and darkly. His twin did not—at least not to the same extent. Along the way, they stopped at a restaurant to get a quick bite to eat. The owner looked them over and then told my uncle, "We'll serve you, but we don't serve spics here."

Ethnic slur aside, my uncle about fell over laughing, given that they were *twins*! But I think it caused my dad to realize in a very personal way the ridiculousness of judging people by the color of their skin and how much it could hurt. He didn't want us raised that way.

My dad was a dockworker at a trucking firm, although he always wanted to be a corporate lawyer. There just wasn't money for that in a family of ten kids, raised during the Depression. He was active in church, he bowled with his friends, and he was an involved father. He instilled a strong sense of the importance of family, perseverance and pride in a job well done. He was strong, stood up for what was right and had a wicked sense of humor.

He (and my mom, of course) bought me my first piano. He had so much faith in my desire to play that he bought a *new* piano. I remember coming home from school that day in fifth grade to see it in the living room. I was ecstatic! For years, driving past the piano store on our way home from church, I dreamed of the day when I would have my own piano, and now here it was. I still have that piano, and music has been and remains a big part of my life. The piano is a reminder of how much they loved me and encouraged my love of music.

My dad died on January 27, and every year, as that date approached, I would start to feel depressed. The actual day was usually a wasted day for me; I just couldn't focus on other things. I did not typically go to his grave on that day because it was *January,* and this is *Iowa*—which means frigid temperatures and snow, making it difficult, if not impossible to even find his grave.

I could not let him go. It seemed disloyal. It wasn't fair. I felt guilty if I wasn't still mourning him. I was the proverbial Daddy's girl—how could I possibly give up that coveted title?

What I am finally realizing is that I don't have to give up my dad. I don't have to give up my memories of him. I don't have to give up my "title." It's like Curt says—I don't have to give up everything; some things I want to keep. But I *do* have to give up the grief that derails me every year. I do not think that my dad would want his death to still be so emotionally crushing this many years later. I need to let go of my anger with God for "taking" him (more on that later), let go of the overwhelming sadness and let go of what could have been.

But what I get to keep is the knowledge that I was *very* loved. I was cherished and wanted in a way that parents who easily conceive children do not experience. I get to keep the memories, the stories and the lessons. I get to keep him in my heart.

And I get to keep his bowling shirt.

CHAPTER 12

MY MOM

There is a pastor at a church I attended who, when he spoke of his parents, always prefaced his story with, "I love my dad, but..." or, "I love my mom, but..." These don't come off as humorous introductions to a quirky story of endearment. They feel more like they're designed to distance himself from his parents ("I'm not like *them*") while at the same time being a "good" son, reassuring us that he loves his parents, despite their eccentricities.

I never start off stories about my dad that way. He died when I was still in the "hero-worship, daddy's-little-girl" stage. I never got to the "I'm an all-knowing teenager, and you're the know-*nothing* dad" stage with him. So there are no qualifiers about my love for him. There is a period after "I love(d) my dad." Not a comma.

With my mom, though, it's a little different story. She *did* live long enough to experience my wonderful teen years! But it's not just that. My mom and I were so different in many respects that one of my teachers, who later became a good friend of my mom's, once remarked that if someone threw a bunch of mothers and daughters together in the room and asked her to match them up, she would *never* have put my mom and me together. That's not to say that one or the other of us was a "better" person—we were just very different.

For example, I once owned a Ford Mustang. It was, unfortunately, the ugly model year, but it was still a *Mustang*. When things changed in my life, I decided I needed to sell it. My mom tried to dissuade me from that, saying, "But you *love* that car!"

My response? "But I can't *afford* that car right now." I sold it and have never regretted that decision.

My mom was also an extrovert—I'm an introvert. My dad once joked that my mom would talk to a fencepost if she thought it would speak back to her. And she laughed right along, knowing he was right. And everyone loved my mom—I tend to be a little slower to warm up to people, again because I'm an introvert (*not* because I am stuck up).

Another difference was more generational than anything else. My mom, like many in her generation, had very traditional ideas about gender roles (and remember, she was significantly older than most of my friends' moms). Once, when Randy and I were at her house, she told me I should "serve" him a piece of pie (pie is another one of those generational things). In no uncertain terms, I told her that if I wanted to take a piece of pie to Randy because I loved him and it was a nice thing to do, I would happily do it. But I would *not* "serve" him *anything* simply because I was the wife and it was my job to serve my "man." She rolled her eyes in disgust—I was a terrible wife in her eyes.

And then there was the evening she came to dinner at our house. As she was leaving, she said in a rush, "I feel like you've always blamed me for your dad's death!"

And then she bolted.

There are not too many times I am speechless, but this was one of them. I was rooted to the spot on the stairs in the garage, wondering what in the *world* she was talking about. My dad died of a heart attack—how could she possibly be responsible for that? I'm sorry to say I never finished that conversation with her. She left so quickly, and I never brought it up again. Even now, when I think of it, I find myself shaking my head, wondering what I had done that could possibly have given her that impression.

I'm not a psychologist, but if I had to guess, I probably pulled away from her after my dad died, not because I blamed her for my dad's death, but instead out of fear. When you love someone and they go away, it is excruciatingly painful. My 12-year-old self probably decided that the "solution" was to not care about people so deeply. Then it wouldn't hurt so much when they died or otherwise left.

As a child, I didn't yet understand that when you miss the pain, you also miss, as the song says, the dance. And you don't understand that your experience with a parent's death as a child is much different than your experience as an adult, primarily because you're not afraid for your very survival when you're an adult. You don't worry about who will take care of you; in fact, for many people, the caregiving roles have switched.

When my mother died, two weeks before my 40th birthday, I received a card from a former neighbor. She wrote, "40 is much too young to lose your mother." I remember feeling a bit surprised at that realization, thinking, "You know, that's true, but it beats the heck out of 12."

My experience with my mother's death was also quite different, and caused me considerably less trauma. For one thing, of course, I was an adult, not a child. But her death was also not as big a surprise as my dad's. The year before she died, she had been diagnosed with kidney cancer. I remember sitting with my mom in the doctor's office when the diagnosis came in. She didn't say a word, but her hands, clasped in front of her on her lap, told the story. Her thumbs were working furiously, circling each other, round and round, in a dance of pure terror. However, the doctor went on to reassure her.

He believed that the tumor was fully encapsulated within her kidney, so there was an easy solution—simply remove the kidney. Which he did. No chemo, no radiation—just surgery. She recovered well, and everyone breathed a sigh of relief. There was one little hiccup, though, that later proved important.

Mom had been diagnosed with diabetes about the same time the tumor showed up in tests. My mother was morbidly obese (a clinical diagnosis, not a personal opinion), so although there wasn't a history of diabetes in her family, I wasn't terribly surprised. She did not have to have insulin shots, but she did take medication. After the surgery, they administered her insulin through an injection because she hadn't awakened from the anesthesia enough to take a pill. And it nearly put her into a coma.

Her sugar plummeted to a breathtaking 25 mg/DL. To put that in context, a normal, fasting glucose reading in a person without diabetes is 70—100 mg/DL. As it turned out, once the tumor was removed, she no longer needed to be treated for diabetes.

About a year later, though, her sugars were out of line again. She called me one day and said, "I think the cancer's back." I asked her why she thought that, but she really couldn't give me a specific reason. Ultimately, I suggested we go see the doctor and get things checked, because I knew that if we didn't, she would just worry about it until we did. Might just as well go now to give her some peace of mind.

She had already seen her family doctor for a routine exam (which resulted in the renewal of her treatment for diabetes), and he had taken a chest X-ray, which was clear. I called and scheduled an appointment with the surgeon, which did *not* go well. He scolded my mother for wasting his time—her cancer wasn't back, and she had no reason to think it was. Why were we even there?

After sitting there watching my mom quietly "take it," I finally leaned forward and, eyes flashing (I am my father's daughter), said, "we are *here* because she's worried the cancer is back, and she wants you to check and see whether that is true." He apparently heard the steel in my voice, and realized that while my mother might sit there quietly without challenging him, that was *not* my personality. He backed off a bit and reassured us that the cancer was not back.

And then two weeks later, she was in the hospital.

I don't remember why we originally took her in, but while there, she had an MRI that showed a mass in the same vicinity as the removed kidney. Her cancer *was* back. She had been right, and the doctor had been wrong. I was furious with him, primarily because he had been so dismissive of her concerns. So I called him. And it was one of the few times that I was absolutely thrilled to call myself a lawyer.

When I called, the receptionist answered. I told her I wanted to speak to Dr. Todd. She asked if she could take my information and have him return my call, which I expected. I told her that I would be happy to give her that information, but—and I was quite clear about this—I wanted to hear back from the doctor—*not* his nurse. Of course, that request was totally ignored.

When the nurse called, I said (rather rudely, I confess), "I told the receptionist I didn't want to talk to you—I want to talk to the doctor."

She told me the doctor was in a meeting "all day long," and wouldn't be available to call me back until early evening or perhaps even the next day. She asked if she could help me or give him a message. I said, "Yes, you can give him a message—'failure to diagnose.'"

Guess who called me less than 15 minutes later?

I told the doctor that he had been wrong, that my mother *did* have cancer. He became defensive, saying, "I did an X-ray, and..."

I angrily cut him off, saying, "*You* didn't order that. Her primary care physician ordered it." It was a small point, but I was not in the mood to let him off the hook for anything. He conceded that point, and told me that he had *reviewed* the X-ray, and it was clear. Because that's where cancer usually reappears, he didn't bother to look anywhere else.

I was tired of his attitude, so I simply said this: "Well, I'm not a doctor. I'm a *lawyer*. But it seems to me that when a patient presents with exactly the same symptoms she had before, you *might* want to check a little further."

And with that, he immediately switched to the script his medical malpractice carrier likely had given him.

I had no intention of suing him (and never threatened a lawsuit), because even if he had diagnosed her when he saw her, the two weeks would not have made a difference. But I wanted him to think about how he was treating people who came to see him, people who were frightened and overwhelmed, and looking to their doctor for reassurance and help. I wanted his bedside manner to change, and for him to be more compassionate.

A different surgeon—one highly respected in his field—talked to Mom about surgery, but because of her weight, she could never get her respiratory functions to a place where surgery would be safe.

There was one event while she was in the hospital, though, that my mother didn't find humorous, but for anyone who knew my mom, caused them to laugh in recognition of who she was—and wasn't.

Her birthday was October 9. On October 8, I went to see her, and she was in a *mood*, which was not really like her. I asked her what had happened, and she told me that her regular doctor had talked to her about making a decision. Either decision she made was fine, but if she wanted to get better, she was going to have to decide to do that, and commit to doing what the doctors were telling her in order to get to where she could have the surgery. My mom took that to mean she was going to die (naturally). So she said to the doctor, "Well! Thanks for ruining my *birthday!*" She looked at me so triumphantly—she had finally stood up for herself.

And I had to burst her bubble. I looked at her and said, "Today's not your birthday."

"It's not?" she said, incredulous.

"No," I responded. "It's tomorrow." Her next response was classic.

"Don't tell the doctor," she said, conspiratorially. And it was all I could do not to burst out laughing, because, of course, her birthday was clearly marked on every document in her chart *and* on her wristband. It's not like we were going to be able to keep this a secret! But she was so proud of herself for standing up to the doctor that I simply agreed not to "tell."

Three days later, on a Sunday morning, I was at home getting ready for church. I taught sixth-grade Sunday School and was thinking about my lesson while drying my hair. The hospital called and "suggested" I might want to get down there relatively soon. (By the way—in case you don't know this—when a hospital suggests this, it is not *really* a suggestion. You need to go, and go quickly). So I went. I hung out with my mom and the nurses all day long.

I tried repeatedly to call my Aunt Marilyn in Wisconsin to tell her that mom wasn't doing well, but she never answered. And then she and Uncle Dick walked through the door. Uncle Dick later told me that Aunt Marilyn would get an update from me and worry. He would ask if she wanted to come to Des Moines. She would say, "No, not yet." Finally, the night before, after my call, he didn't ask. He just told her to pack so they could leave in the morning. I was so glad they came down. Mom never really regained consciousness that day, although I think she knew Marilyn was there. She opened her eyes a few times, but never spoke.

She died that evening around 7 o'clock with her family around her. My phone rang five minutes later, and I saw that it was the same pastor who had been at my bedside when I first learned of my father's death. I stepped out in the hall and took his call. I had left him a message the day before, asking if he might be able to come visit. He was retired but still did some hospital visitations for Grace Church. Mom wasn't a member there, but I thought perhaps because of our long association, he might come, especially if he was already at the hospital.

He had only picked up my message a few minutes earlier, however. I told him that mom had just died, and although I don't recall his exact words, his compassion was evident. After I hung up, I realized that he broke the news to me about my dad dying, and I broke the news to him about mom dying, which was rather surreal.

I also understood for the first time in my life what the picture of a candle on a hospital door meant.

I had trouble falling asleep that night, and then in the middle of the night, the phone rang, frightening me—had something *else* happened? Middle-of-the-night calls are not usually good news. But it was only the funeral home, asking if I wanted her body embalmed. I told the man I had no idea—what was normally done, and why? He explained that if the funeral was more than a certain number of days after the death, state law required embalming. That being the case, I didn't know why he was calling. The funeral was clearly going to be outside that window of time, and he had woken me up after I had barely fallen asleep to ask me a question that had only one answer. Couldn't the call have waited until morning?

As adult children (and with my mother having no surviving spouse), it fell to my younger brother and me to make all the arrangements. There were people to call, flowers and a casket to buy, clothes to pick out, musicians to line up and stories to tell the pastor. At the time, I had both a landline and a cell phone, and many times was on both simultaneously. I don't really remember much about those intervening days, just a snippet or two here and there that make no sense now, out of context.

After the visitation (which, for an introvert like me is exhausting, despite the beautiful words of comfort and memories), there is the funeral, followed by the gravesite service. I didn't want limousines—that still reminded me too much of my dad's death. So we borrowed a Sequoia from Randy's brother Jeff and his wife Pam. Two of my cousins, Mike and Ron, were serving as pallbearers and rode with us. They are broad-shouldered, big men who completely filled the middle seat; they are the size (and temperament, frankly) that you would want on your side in a fight. But at one point, I called back, "Logan! Are you still back there?" He was in the "way back," and I couldn't see him through the wall of my two protectors.

Ron later told me that when he saw me walking back to the vehicle after the gravesite service, all he could think was, "She is *so* done." But of course, I wasn't done. There was still the luncheon to attend, and friends and family to thank and talk to. All that busyness serves to keep you distracted until you crash into bed the day after the funeral and do nothing but sleep fitfully.

Although I had significantly more responsibilities when my mom died than when my dad did, the support I received following my mom's death felt more normal. When you are a child and a parent dies, no one really knows what to do, so they do anything and everything just to try to make you not hurt so much. When you're an adult, it's still about acknowledging the pain, but supporting you in a different way.

I am grateful to the people who helped get me through it all. To my cousin, Fred, for flying all the way from Washington State to serve as a pallbearer. Originally, he and his wife Peggy were not planning to come back. But when I expressed disappointment, telling him that Mom had wanted him to be a pallbearer, he simply said, "Then I will be there. Whatever Aunt Edith wants, she gets." And he promptly flew back to serve. I still cry when I think of that simple, yet overwhelming act of generosity.

To my friend Tracy, who made sure there was food for us at the visitation. To Angie, who called and said, "I would like to bring dinner." Before I could protest that it was not necessary, she followed up with, "Please say yes."

To the nurses who stayed close to both my mom *and* me in her last hours. To Marilyn and Dick, who had the intuition that it was time to come. To Reverend Henry, who called, and Mary Bramer, who got to the hospital so fast after I called that she must have been going double the posted speed limit. And to many, many other people—those who showed up, brought food and generally supported us in whatever way we needed.

Ultimately, my mom was ready to go. You could tell there was some reluctance when she would look at pictures of her grandkids. Yet she was tired and just didn't want to put in the Herculean effort it would have taken her to get well. I later learned that she had been talking about being "ready to go see Albert." Just before she died, her eyes opened wide, and I wondered what she was seeing and experiencing. Was it my dad? Was it heaven? She couldn't tell me, of course, and in a moment she was gone.

But the biggest difference between my mom's death and my dad's? I got to say goodbye. I had time to tell her I loved her. I was allowed to let her go *gently*.

CHAPTER 13
MISTAKES

I am a person who has always *hated* making mistakes or being wrong. When I was in the fourth grade, we were having our weekly spelling bee. When it was my turn, my teacher, Mrs. Bennett (a favorite of mine), perched on the edge of her desk, wound her legs into their signature knot, and dramatically said, "Oh, I can *never* fool her!" And immediately, the pressure was on to get it *right*, to live up to that image of never making a spelling mistake.

And you guessed it—I missed the very next word she gave me.

I was *mortified*, and I'm sure Mrs. Bennett felt terrible, too. She would never have intentionally embarrassed me. I sat down quickly and pretended to read a book so my classmates couldn't see my tears. I had failed. I had been wrong, which made me desperately unhappy. Maybe I *wasn't* really "the smart girl." But if I wasn't the smart girl, who was I? I certainly wasn't the pretty one in fourth grade, with my braces and octagonal glasses!

I hadn't outgrown this need to be right by law school, going so far as to develop strategies to not be wrong. In Constitutional Law, for example, we had a professor who took great delight in demonstrating how smart he was and how smart we weren't. We used to joke that not only did we not know the answer; we weren't even sure what the *question* was! I quickly learned to volunteer when I did know the answer, so he was less likely to call on me when I *didn't*. I am pleased to report, however, that in a moment of epic karma, this professor was "schooled" by Justice Scalia in a faculty luncheon. Oh, to have been a fly on *that* wall.

And I was already planning how to minimize "being wrong" after law school. I had a conversation with a friend who urged me to work in the area of criminal law. He reminded me that defendants had a constitutional right to counsel. I told him that I knew that, of course, but that did *not* mean they had a right to have *me* as their counsel.

The truth (which I admit freely) is that I was afraid of making a mistake when the stakes were so high. If you lose a civil case, about the only thing your client loses is money. In criminal law, he stands to lose his freedom and perhaps even his life. I didn't want to be responsible for that. Nor did I want to be responsible (as a prosecutor) for sending someone to prison who was innocent. While there are other reasons why criminal law would not have been a good fit for me (I have enough nightmares without viewing grisly evidence from a murder scene, for example), the primary one was my fear of making a mistake.

The problem is, when you don't make mistakes, you don't learn as much. Worse yet, you get stuck with the label of "never making mistakes," which means that when you *do* make a mistake (which you will), people make a big deal out of it. And then you start pulling back, because you don't *like it* when people make a big deal out of your mistakes! You stick with what you know; you stay where it's safe. You might continue to be right, but you will not long be happy.

I finally decided it was more important for me to be happy and to learn than it was to be right and never grow. When I "adopted" Curt as my mentor, I had an initial meeting with a client that he was going to observe and critique. After she left, but before Curt could offer his suggestions, I said to him, "I want you to tell me the truth. I don't want you to be mean about it, of course, but I'm more concerned with improving than I am of having my little feelings protected."

He looked at me for a long minute, seeming to assess whether I really meant that, and then proceeded to, shall we say, test my commitment to that statement! He told me the truth. I later observed him critique others, people who made the exact same mistakes I did, and not point out those mistakes, because they had not asked him to tell them the truth. I was able to grow faster than others at the firm because I was willing to acknowledge my mistakes and correct them.

However.

Part of the reason I was able to hear what Curt had to say to me—and accept it—was because I trusted the relationship. I knew that whatever he said to me was designed to help me, not hurt me—even in those rare times when it *did* sting a bit (learning to manage *that* was a growth opportunity in and of itself). I cannot say the same about trusting a former boss. Whether that is true or not (i.e., his intention was to hurt, not help) is another question. But whereas I was open to hearing whatever Curt had to say and to seriously consider it, I was *not* open to what my boss had to say. I didn't trust that relationship because of past behavior.

When my former boss, Bill, hired me, the company was in the process of building a new wing. Until that was open, people were practically stacked on top of each other. I was given a cubicle, but Bill said I would have an office once the new wing opened up. Now, this is a promise I would remember. I'd be lying if I said that it wasn't about prestige at all, but the main point is that I don't work well in a cube. I'm too distracted by what's going on around me, I worry about distracting others when I'm on the phone or talking to someone in my cube, and there's no sense of privacy.

People just walk right in and start talking, even if you're deep in thought about a project.

Unfortunately, he didn't keep his word. And not only did he not keep his word, but he also didn't *tell* me I wasn't getting an office. Instead, I found out when the new seating chart came out. I was furious. Ultimately, he told me that the decision had come from higher up on the food chain, which is entirely possible. But I told him that he still should have *told* me. And he agreed. Unfortunately, his actions told me that I couldn't trust him to keep his word. From there on out, anything he told me was met with at least some skepticism about whether he would do what he said he would do.

But it wasn't just about keeping his word. There was another time when I sequestered myself in a conference room with no windows for a two-hour period and created the strategic plan for my department. I wrote it all out on those poster-sized Post-It® notes, hung all around the room. When I was done, I invited Bill to come in and showed him my work. He was mildly complimentary, but *I* knew it was good work. So after he left, I pulled them all down and hung them in my consolation-prize-bigger-cubicle (and I may or may not have rolled my eyes, too).

A bit later, Bill came by and asked if the could "borrow" my plan. He didn't say what he wanted to do with it, but he was my boss, so I agreed. As I later walked through the office, I passed by the boardroom and saw *my* plan on the wall, with Bill presenting it to the CEO and the COO. Now, it's unlikely that he was trying to take credit for creating it (it was in my handwriting, after all), but the fact that he didn't include me or even tell me what he was doing was again, infuriating.

Those are the types of actions that destroy trust. And so, when he had a criticism, even if it was legitimate, I wasn't willing to listen, because he had not demonstrated that he was looking out for my best interests. He was looking out for *his* best interests. That, in turn, created a culture where everyone was in constant CYA mode, unable to work as a team, because we were always questioning people's motives.

With Curt, it was much easier to admit when I was wrong, because I knew his corrections were designed to help me become, as one blogger humorously wrote, "100% right—eventually." It can be incredibly difficult to swallow your pride and admit your part in a bad situation. But I've found that it is also empowering. If I've played a role in creating the problem, I can also play a role in solving it. If I can admit I was wrong, I can learn and grow, instead of staying stuck in safe mode, just treading water, never going anywhere. I can't control what other people are doing, but I *can* control my response and *my* actions.

When I recently read John Ortberg's book *All the Places to Go: How Will You Know?*, I found it's a great book for people like me, who struggle to always make the *right* decision. One comment struck a particular chord with me. He writes, "[V]ery often God's will for you will be 'I want *you* to decide,' because decision making is an indispensible part of character formation...This means a new way of looking at life...*I no longer have to live under the tyranny of the perfect choice.*" And that's what it has been for me in my "no-mistake zone"—a tyranny. He also notes that the open door—an opportunity—is "symbolic of ... *unlimited* chances to do something worthwhile."

Those chances can only be unlimited *if* mistakes aren't fatal—and they rarely are. Writing this book was so difficult because it highlights *a lot* of mistakes I've made—and tried to keep hidden in my quest to be "perfect." But it has been a great opportunity to empty the sludge out of my life bucket so I can refill it with sparkling clean water. I can't move forward if I'm always trying to hide what's gone before, because I have to constantly monitor my conversation. *Does she know about the foreclosure?* I think as I'm trying *not* to explain why we live where we currently do. *Is my fear of making a mistake obvious to my opposing counsel? She'll eat me alive!* I worry as my heart starts racing at the start of a hearing.

That doesn't mean I'm going to *dwell* on my mistakes—that's not helpful, either. It just means I'm going to acknowledge them, learn from them and move on. I'm going to take the people with me who know who I am and care about me anyway. And I don't have to bury my face in a book, hiding my tears and my shame over making a mistake. I can start working on displacing the sludge with water.

Done. (And the bonus is that now I have "filling the bucket" material for my next book. I can hardly *wait* to get started on that one!)

CHAPTER 14
CONNECTIONS

I'm reading a book about tidying. The author claims that, if you follow her method, you will only have to do it once. After that, it's just a matter of putting things back where they belong. One main point? Keep only those things that "spark joy."

The TV show *What Not to Wear,* on the other hand, resorts to bribery. In order to get the $5,000 gift card for a new wardrobe *and* a hair *and* make-up makeover, you have to agree to turn your entire current wardrobe over to the hosts, who will most likely ruthlessly throw it all out (because let's face it—if you had great clothes, you wouldn't be on the show in the first place).

Another method regarding clothes is to throw out anything you haven't worn in the last six months. This, however, does not work particularly well in climates with wild temperature swings between the seasons—like Iowa.

Finally, William Morris advises us to, "Have nothing in your house that you do not know to be useful, or believe to be beautiful."

Yet there is one other reason I hang on to certain things; things that seem to have no real purpose in my life, or that are inconsistent with my style.

As I've written before, the night before my dad died, he went bowling. I still have his orange bowling shirt (minus the Iowa Power and Light sponsor patch—I'm not sure what happened to that). If I were ever a contestant on *What Not to Wear*, I would hide that shirt from Stacey London. If she found it, I would be tempted to give up the wardrobe, the hair makeover and the makeup session, all to hang onto that shirt. Well—I might not go that far, but it would be a tough call.

I have a Younkers charge card with my dad's signature, a name-etag, his glasses and some other odds and ends. I really have no idea why those things were retained, or where any of the other equally miscellaneous things ended up. I have a small table he built, his metal workbench and the cupboards and baby crib he built for me.

The things he built, the things with his writing on them (including canceled checks), and the things most closely associated with my memories of him (like the bowling shirt and his metal workbench) are things I hang onto. They have moved with me from house to house to house. Even when we lost our house on Glenwood, those things went with me. Non-negotiable.

These are more than just memories. They are concrete things he touched, created and, in a sense, blessed. They make me feel connected to him in a different way than a simple memory or story.

When someone dies, there is sometimes a fight over possessions. People accuse one another of being greedy, and sometimes that *is* what's going on. But for me, the things, whether big or small, are the connections to the loved one that has died. They help me hold tightly to his memory and help me further share that memory with my children. Because my children obviously never met their grandfather, sharing his *things* helps me tell his story and make him more "real" in their eyes. Kind of like the Alamo, although on an obviously much smaller scale. Reading about it is one thing;

going there, standing on that hallowed ground and looking at the artifacts is something completely different.

When my mom died, it was up to my brother and me to go through her things. Besides the usual three piles (keep, donate, throw away), there was a fourth pile—the "I'm not sure yet" pile. This pile tended to have functional items that I would not likely ever use, but were associated with a strong memory of her. From a practical standpoint, they would have been easy to get rid of, but from an emotional standpoint, they were not.

What I found was that although I wasn't ready to get rid of them right then, after a year had passed, I *was* ready to let go of many of them. I was in a better place to objectively decide what would mean the most to me. If I had not allowed myself that time and space, instead limiting myself to the three categories, I might have had regrets about tossing things. The things I kept purely for memory included handwritten recipe cards, (when my kids used the card with her lemon bar recipe, they had to ask what "oleo" was), her childhood tea set, and the popcorn bowl.

The recipes I kept because I'm such a word person that almost anything with handwriting on it is something I will keep. But they also reminded me of the food that Mom prepared, whether for immediate family meals or extended family potlucks. The childhood tea set was different, because there *was* no memory associated with that. In fact, I don't remember ever seeing it. It had been packed away, probably to keep it safe. It appeared to be missing a few pieces already. Tea sets back then, even children's tea sets, were glass, not plastic. My mom always loved "pretty dishes," and I would guess this beautiful little green tea set started that love affair.

But what could be special about a popcorn bowl? In fact, it wasn't technically a popcorn bowl; it was her large mixing bowl, and it was part of a colorful set that many women of her generation had. The largest bowl, the "popcorn" bowl, was yellow, but there was also a smaller green one. They were apparently not dishwasher safe, because some of the color of the green one had come off. But it wasn't really about the bowl itself, but rather what it represented.

On Friday nights when I was a child and my dad was still living, we would play Monopoly®. At a certain point, my mom would go bankrupt. I suspect it was intentional, when it was nearing bedtime. She would get up and, while the rest of us continued to play, make popcorn. There was always plenty of butter and salt, and it seems like we were also allowed a pop (probably grape or strawberry), although that might not be right. Perhaps Kool-Aid? In any event, once the popcorn was done, it was time to put away the game, whether it was over or not. We would each get our own cereal-bowl of popcorn, and when it was gone, it was time to brush our teeth and head to bed, a bit later than usual. Friday nights were such a special treat, and the popcorn bowl reminds me of those times.

I also discovered that some of the gadgets she loved—ones I had previously scoffed at (who needs an electric *apple peeler*?)— turned out to be quite useful (like the aforementioned apple peeler). Other things were both functional *and* gave me a peek into the social part of her life and the lives of her peers. For example, she had a fair amount of Tupperware® and Pampered Chef® items. When I was growing up, women often went to these kinds of home parties. It provided a social event, to be sure, but by agreeing to host parties, they helped each other get things they might not otherwise have been able to afford. If you booked a party while attending a party, the hostess received free gifts and/or points to use toward products. With a family the size of my dad's (ten kids), you can imagine how many parties could sprout up from one!

Home Interiors®, another home party-based business, was another favorite, and I still have a print of a young girl that my mom purchased for my bedroom when I was growing up. She used to buy their wrought-iron sconces, which I didn't care for while I was young. Yet now I find myself drawn to wrought iron, albeit in a much different style. My mom loved frou-frou, frilly things, but

I did not. I was more into clean lines, and sometimes even rustic items. Things that were sturdy rather than delicate and fragile. Needless to say, I did *not* keep the white plastic butterflies that she bought from Home Interiors®!

The experience of holding onto things for a year or so before giving them away also helped me in a different way a few years later.

My mother-in-law suffered from dementia in her later years. At a certain point, it became clear that she was not going to be able to live alone in her condo any longer. She was going to have to give up her driver's license and sell her car (to her youngest son, Tim. But poor Tim—he bought the car, and she later told people he stole it! Dementia is a horrible thing).

Martha moved into a one-bedroom apartment in an assisted living facility. Needless to say, she no longer needed all the "stuff" she had in her larger condo. But dementia made it difficult for her to let go of things. I suspect that it was too much change all at once, and perhaps the items helped her remember. In any event, my sister-in-law, who is very practical, was getting a bit frustrated because Martha was trying to hang onto too many things that she would likely never use. Remembering how I had felt about my mom's things, I finally spoke up and suggested that we simply box up those items and store them in our garage. If, after a year, she hadn't asked about them or needed them, we could then donate them.

It was a beautiful solution. It reduced Martha's stress (and we didn't tell her about the one-year deadline; she wouldn't have remembered anyway) because we weren't forcing her to part with things that were meaningful to her, but yet had no real use at this stage in her life. And it reduced Pam's frustration because she didn't have to "persuade" Martha to let go of those things, and we didn't have to try to find a spot for them in the new place. They wouldn't have to be sorted through again at a later date—they could just be donated.

I sometimes feel like we hasten death when we don't allow people to make as many decisions as they can, or when we do too many things for them, reversing the trend of helicopter parents by becoming helicopter children. Whether under the guise of trying to be helpful, or if we are just trying to be efficient for our own sake, we inadvertently make people feel like they no longer have any control over their life. They feel useless and a burden and just give up. No matter our age, we all need to feel needed. We all need to have at least some sense of control in our life.

I've also learned that sometimes we don't know the history of an item, so we don't understand the resistance to letting it go. Because we are only looking at the "popcorn bowl" and its usefulness (or lack thereof), we miss the more compelling reason driving our desire to keep it.

One of the things Randy brought to our marriage all those years ago was a television set. It wasn't anything special—just a TV. When it started having problems, we purchased a new one, but he didn't seem too motivated to let go of the broken one. Finally, in exasperation, I asked him why we were keeping it. It was analog, it didn't work, and it was big and bulky.

It turned out he had purchased that television set with the money he received after his dad died. Since I hadn't yet met Randy when his dad died, I didn't know that. To me, it was just a television set. To him, it was a link to his dad. I stopped pushing to get rid of it, and eventually, when he was ready, he let it go.

Deciding what to keep, what to donate and what to throw away isn't always a simple as asking if something brings you "joy," if you've worn it in the last six months, or even if is particularly useful or beautiful. Sometimes it's about the memory and the connection.

And sometimes, we hold on tightly to that thing that connects us and has meaning for us—even if it makes no sense to anyone else. And that's okay.

CHAPTER 15

MEMORIES

As I noted in the previous chapter, my mother-in-law suffered from dementia, although it was lung cancer that ultimately took her life. Oddly enough, when she received her cancer diagnosis, she was lucid enough to say, "Well *that's* not good news." Her "lung doctor" took her small hands into his NBA-sized ones, and gently asked her if she had smoked. She nodded, and he did, too, quite compassionately. She had quit smoking several years back, but not soon enough, it appeared.

Arrangements were made for hospice to begin visiting, and our own visits to Martha increased. I remember putting lotion on her freshly manicured hands (hospice is wonderful about "spoiling" their patients), swabbing the inside of her mouth to keep it moist and putting lip balm on her chapped lips. Interesting the things you remember, isn't it?

In some respects, the dementia eased the emotional part of cancer for her, because her memory of the diagnosis left her at about the same time we left the doctor's office.

Dementia causes different behaviors in different people, and in Martha, the dementia caused her to repeat conversations over and over—within a very short time frame. When we would go visit her, we would make small talk, about the weather, perhaps. There would be a brief "transitional" silence, but rather than move to a different conversation, she would repeat the one she just had. It was as though she was stuck in this infinite conversation loop and couldn't extricate herself from it.

It did have odd moments of humor, though, and was one of the few times in my life I felt okay about lying. One day, I was visiting her in the assisted living apartment where she resided, and as I got ready to leave, I said, "I'll see you on Monday."

"I'm not going to be here," she replied. I was reaching for the door but stopped and turned to look at her, to see if she was joking. She was not. I was pretty sure she didn't have a doctor's appointment on Monday (my sister-in-law and I coordinated those, providing transportation), and by and large, her social life didn't exist outside the visitors who showed up at her apartment. Curious, I asked, "Where are you going?"

"To court," she informed me. Now she had my attention. I walked back into the room to hear the story. She explained that her youngest son, Tim, had broken into her previously owned condo and was staying in the basement. She had to go testify against him.

Now, clearly this wasn't true. The condo didn't even *have* a basement! And, of course, Tim wasn't living there or anywhere other than his own place. I suspected that the new meds she was on were causing either vivid dreams or hallucinations. I tried to explain this to her, and she nodded in agreement, and then went right back to the loop of going to court. Finally, in an effort to break that loop, I said, "You're not going to court on Monday," and held my breath.

"Why not?" she asked. "Did the case get dismissed?"

"Yes," I replied without batting an eye. Yes, it was a lie; one I told with a complete lack of remorse. That seemed to get her out of the loop and calm her. I mean, really—what mother wants to testify against her son?

Communication was difficult for a variety of reasons. One was the infinite loop, but other challenges included her inability to sometimes find the right words and to distinguish what was real from hallucinations. She once took a nasty spill in her apartment, falling out of her wheelchair. No one was there at the time, and when we asked her what had happened, she said she tripped over a tricycle. Whether she meant wheelchair, or whether she really believed there was a tricycle in her apartment, the result was the same—neither she nor any of us could figure out what actually happened.

New research seems to suggest that the sense of smell may be an early indicator of cognitive decline and subsequent memory loss. As I think back on Martha's journey, I remember that she did, in fact, lose her sense of smell, but we thought it was just from all the years of smoking. It's a sense that we don't often think about, yet it's one of the most powerful ways to instantly take us back to a memory.

For example, the smell of lilacs will forever remind me of the bush we had in our yard when I was growing up. Every year, my brother and I would take a bouquet to our teachers. This was a bit of a challenge because of the water issue. Mom would wrap the stems in a wet paper towel and put the whole thing in a "baggie." This was before zip-lock styles, however, so the baggie sometimes got lost in transit, leaving us holding soggy paper towels and dripping all over our homework assignments.

I remember one year in particular. I was a sophomore in high school and took a bunch of the fragrant blooms to my geometry teacher, Mr. Floyd Lancaster. "F.L." (as he was known to his students) teared up. I don't know if he had a special memory attached to lilacs or whether he was just touched that a high school student would bring him flowers. I suspect elementary school teachers are more often the recipient of flowers from their students than are high school teachers. Whatever the reason, it earned me a special place in his heart (although it did not help my geometry grade).

Memories are *so* important, yet often we don't know when we're making them. Sure, the big vacations will create great memories, but often it's the smaller things that make us smile wistfully. And I am often touched to learn, after the fact, the things that were important to others. Little things that I gave scarce thought to, but which were remembered months, or even years later.

My niece and nephew go to a school that hosts a Grandparent's Day each year. Unfortunately for them, they have only one living grandparent, and he does not "do" school events like that, for whatever reason. So I have traditionally stood in as the "fabulous aunt." This year, McKenzie's class filled out a paper talking about their grandparent (or, in her case, aunt). One of the things was, "The best thing she cooks is." McKenzie's answer puzzled me, because she had written "cheesecake." I didn't remember ever making cheesecake for her, so I asked about it. She reminded me that in December, she had visited me for a Christmas baking and crafts day. One of the things we made together was cheesecake in a jar (the recipe is on Pinterest—it's fabulous!).

It occurred to me that her answer was less about the cheesecake than it was about the experience of *making* the cheesecakes together. We had great fun, and she was a great helper. For the crafts part, we made bird seed wreaths (those did *not* turn out as well as the cheesecakes, even for the birds), and she painted a picture frame ornament. I took a selfie of the two of us, printed it and put it into her picture frame ornament, a reminder of our fun day together. The last sentence on her school paper reflects the importance of these small things. In response to the writing prompt, "As you can see, my aunt is very special because," McKenzie wrote, "She ♥s me."

And it's true, I do "♥" her. And because both of her paternal grandparents are deceased, I try very hard to create some of the memories she would have otherwise had with them. I go to soccer games and baseball/softball games and Grandparent's Day. I have baking days and "field trip" days with them (the Science Center was a big hit). I cross-stitch Christmas stockings for them that will be here long after I am gone, and will hopefully serve as a reminder of how much I love them.

Martha may not have remembered the things she did with her boys or her grandkids, but *they* remember. They can still tell the stories. They can keep her memory alive by talking about her and the things she did. Making—and sharing—memories reminds us that we are better together, and that ultimately, it's all about relationships. It's important to carry those memories from generation to generation, weaving together people who may never know—or in some cases remember—each other.

CHAPTER 16

FAMILY

My father came from a family of ten kids—seven boys (including one set of twins) and three girls. At one point, my grandmother had four boys under the age of five, when she was a mere 20 years old herself (this included the set of twins, of which my father was one). This was during the Depression, so things were especially challenging.

My grandfather had only a 5th grade education, but he could do math in his head like nobody's business. Both my brother and my son inherited that. When Logan was in second grade, we were in the car one day when he started "doing math" out loud. "1+1 is 2. 2+2 is 4. 4+4 is 8." He continued doubling until he got to 32,768. *32,768*—in his *head*. At seven years old. He asked if that was right. I had no idea—I was trying to drive, after all (yeah, that's it—I was *driving*).

We are a family who has been deeply involved in military service. Even my grandma did her part, leading the local Navy Mother's group. We have annual Christmas parties (which we hold in a church fellowship hall, because we are too large for anyone's home) that require a planning breakfast at the Machine Shed restaurant in the fall. It used to be a handful of female cousins that met to plan the date, location, Santa's visit, activities for the kids *and* centerpieces, but then Nancy started bringing her husband, whom we referred to as the token male. He persuaded Val's husband Scott to come, so we are now well on our way to gender diversity (insert sarcastic eye roll—*and* the comment that I really *am* glad they come—they add a great deal of fun to the breakfast, despite the fact that Ron always tries to institute a "last one to arrive pays" rule).

We also have picnics in the summer. I remember one summer when I was a child. We often played a rousing game of softball (we had plenty of people for two teams, after all), but I don't know if we were doing that or just generally playing around. In any event, my cousin Larry stepped on a hornet's nest. Oh, my! He began yelling, and his dad grabbed him, tossed him in the car and yanked off his pants (because the insects had flown up his pant legs). That poor kid!

Family life and church life often overlapped. Although my parents had moved "way out west" to Urbandale, a suburb of Des Moines, before I was born, we still attended church on the east side of Des Moines along with some of my family. Not all of us attended Sheridan Park UMC, but we could still fill a pew, and it's where Grandma and Grandpa went to church. It was always a treat to sit further up front with them and watch Grandma nudge Grandpa awake on occasion.

After church, we went to Grandma and Grandpa's house, just a short distance from church. On nice days, we might even be given permission to *walk,* which again, was a treat for us. But when we were in the car, we would inevitably see their neighbor, Mrs. Smith walking home, Bible in hand, striding purposefully in her orthopedic black shoes, best dress and hat. We always offered her a ride, and she always declined. The routine never changed. But it was always important to my parents that we offered. What great role models they were about caring for others!

Other aunts, uncles, and cousins converged on my grandparent's home to share that meal—which, like our routine with Mrs. Smith, also never varied—fried eggs, bacon, toast and orange juice. Everyone brought food to contribute, but no one ever brought anything different. And if you didn't butter the toast *all the way to the edge,* Grandpa would send it back (just ask my cousin Laurie)!

Of course, the dining room wasn't big enough for all of us to eat at the same time, so the kids ate first and then headed outside to play baseball in the side yard (trying desperately to stay out of Grandma's flowerbed), or walked down a short tree-lined path for a visit with Great-Aunt Maggie. The uncles ate next, and then retired to the living room to read the paper and doze. The women ate last, lingering at the table over coffee, visiting. It was Norman Rockwell idyllic.

Like most families, we have lots of stories, although I tend to believe that my family has had perhaps more than its fair share of adventures. I have an uncle who was awarded the Purple Heart for an injury he received on Iwo Jima. I have a cousin who fell off a navy ship (and lived to tell about it). I have an uncle who was in a horrific accident that left his semi flattened, and another who had a motorcycle drive over the top of his car. And those are just the stories I can tell.

Funny stories about travel, vaulting out of hay mows and jumping trains (well, they're funny now, anyway). Touching stories of ice skates and looking for lost brothers and rescuing toddlers on a paper route. Teachable moments, involving losing all your money (7¢) in a poker game (don't gamble), standing up for family (even if you are, at the same time, fighting with them), and telling (and showing) people you love them. I finally decided that my big project for the year is to put them all together in a legacy book. I don't want to lose the stories.

As you might imagine, with a family this size, Grandma and Grandpa couldn't buy us all birthday and Christmas presents every year, or any year, really. But what Grandma did give us has turned out to be more valuable than any toy or game she could have bought for us.

She gave us family photos.

I remember that at parties, weddings and any other family gathering, Grandma would be there with her Brownie box camera, peering down into it, trying to get us to stand still and smile. At Christmas parties, she would take pictures of each family, as well as other group pictures—all the girl cousins and all the boy cousins, for example. Then, a few months later (after the film had been used and developed), we would get an envelope with our name on it that contained the pictures.

I have tried to replicate those "photo shoots" at our Christmas parties, with some success. But I don't have as much pull as Grandma in getting people together—we joke that it's like herding cats to get that many people to "cooperate."

A few years ago, though, my cousins and I decided to create a family photo book. It was quite ambitious because it involved two pages for every family. The page on the left had the wedding picture of the aunt/uncle, surrounded by old family photos of their immediate family. On the right-hand page were the current photos of their progeny.

There were candid pictures in the back and a good-natured (but true) list of what I learned by being raised a Pinegar (my family name). Each family was to do their own pages, but again, the cat herding issue came up, and so some of us ended up doing pages for multiple families. The cousins paid for one book to be given to each of our aunts and uncles. Others could—and did—buy their own copies. The aunts and uncles were so surprised, and, I think, moved. They spent the rest of the party poring over those books.

Two years ago, my Aunt Mickey and Aunt Becky spent time on Ancestry.com and provided each of the families with a more detailed genealogy, going way back to our European ancestors.

Priceless. And then, last year, my daughter took the time to put all of this into a family tree, which my second-cousin Val printed. We hung that on the wall at the Christmas party, and it drew a great deal of interest, as well as starting conversations and reminding people of other stories.

In case you haven't yet caught on, family is important to us.

Now, this doesn't mean it's always sunshine and light. Some in my family have suffered from substance abuse issues, divorce and work or financial issues. We sometimes hurt each other (inadvertently).

Although I am an introvert, I am a rather outspoken one. If I see something wrong, I'm going to talk about it. If I have an opinion about something I see in the news, I'm likely to comment. I don't resort to name calling or hurling insults. I simply present a different point of view and/or ask questions. I don't care if people disagree with me, but I want that disagreement to be based on facts and evidence, not media spin. And I don't always say what *I* believe—I just want people to think about both sides of an issue.

But not everyone appreciates my "challenges"—even some in my family. Most simply scroll past. My brother will occasionally make snarky comments. But one of my cousins actually unfriended me on Facebook. I didn't realize this had happened, though, until I realized it had been a while since I saw a post from her. I went back and looked, and it said we weren't "friends." I assumed it was a technology thing, so I emailed her and asked. There was no response.

Now I was feeling concerned. So I called her at home. Her husband answered, and as he handed her the phone said, "You're busted." I asked her about it, and instead of responding directly, she suggested we have dinner. This was not looking good. My anxiety level was high, and I couldn't imagine what I had done to cause her to take that drastic step.

At dinner, she told me that my posts made her angry. At first, I thought she meant my blog posts, so I said, "Well, why don't you just stop reading them? You don't have to unfriend me!" But then I realized she was talking about my Facebook posts. I would assume she was referring to my political ones, but even so, that bothers me. This country has become very polarized, in large part because we are unwilling to talk to each other about the things that matter. We've forgotten the *real* meaning of tolerance; i.e., being able to accept other people's positions without "acquiring" them.

My cousin said she didn't want me to change, so she thought that rather than confront me about my posts, she would instead quietly unfriend me so she didn't have to see them. She said she loved me. But I have to honestly say, all of that really hurt. I asked her why they made her angry. The only thing she would say (and I'm not sure it was the full truth) was that I challenged her beliefs. I made her think, and she didn't want to think about some of the beliefs she held near and dear.

I like to think I have forgiven her, but I would be lying if I said it doesn't still hurt when I see her. That part, though, I need to let go of. I'm sure I've hurt others in my family—unintentionally. Yet they still love *me*. We're family. We stick together. And despite the hurt, I would still defend her to *anyone* who dared criticize her.

But not everyone is fortunate enough to have a family like mine. For a few years, I served as a Court Appointed Special Advocate. CASAs advocate for children who have been abused or neglected, or when there is concern that they might be. CASAs serve one family at a time, and act as a second set of eyes and ears for the court. We visit our kids every month and help facilitate the process. This is a different role than a *guardian ad litem,* which is the child's *legal* advocate; you do not need to be an attorney to be a CASA. In fact, many teachers make excellent CASAs (usually after they retire from teaching).

My first case involved a family where a child had died while in mom's care (not her child, but a niece). Mom had several kids, all of whom were immediately removed from the home. There were multiple fathers, so one child went with his dad, while the others initially went to foster care. Later, one moved to be with his dad, and finally the remaining children joined him. Such chaos in these little ones' lives! And Dad wasn't a particularly good role model either, having had his own brushes with the law.

Ultimately, mom went to prison for a time in a plea agreement. When I asked one of the dads how he was going to make sure the children maintained contact with their mom, he first said, "They can send letters." And then I reminded him that he would also have to take them to visit her, if the court ordered that. (This is a complex issue, which I'm not going to discuss here, but essentially, there's a delicate balancing act by the court. Regardless of what the parent has done, kids still love their parent and want to see her/him; their mental health needs that contact, yet there is obviously a need to protect them as well). Dad bristled, taking a step toward me, and said he was *not* going to take his children to prison to visit her. This is where you sometimes have to be tough as a CASA—you have to be able to go toe-to-toe with the parents in difficult situations, because you are the *child's* advocate, not the parent's.

I didn't back up, nor did I back down. "If the court orders it, you *will* allow that, or you will find yourself in contempt," I responded firmly. I do not particularly like confrontations like this, but my family has taught me to stand up for myself (and others), which has stood me in good stead.

It turned out that the reason he was pushing back so strongly on this had nothing to do with his kids. He was not allowed in the women's prison because of his own legal issues, which meant that his *new* wife had to take his kids from a previous marriage to visit his *ex*-wife in prison.

I'm sure that went over well.

The cases were so heartbreaking. I had a preschooler who could "imitate" what a dead baby looked like (trust me—you do not want to see this). I had a little boy who just looked like a lost soul. And a tough-on-the-outside girl who scribbled, "I love my mom" over every square inch of her notebook. Once, she and I were kicking a soccer ball around in her yard. She gave me one of those looks and deliberately kicked it into the neighbor's yard, and then ordered me to "go get it." I just laughed and said, "No—*you* kicked it over there, so you need to go get it."

Surprisingly, she didn't argue with me, but instead started over to get the ball. I decided that maybe I should go with her, so I started walking that direction, too. She stopped in her tracks, looked at me menacingly and said, "Don't you touch me!"

I stopped and said very calmly, "I'm not going to touch you. I'm just going to go with you to get the ball." Her body visibly relaxed, and she simply said, "Oh." We went on to retrieve the ball, but I wondered what had happened to her to cause a reaction like that.

Being a CASA was an eye-opening experience. It made me appreciate my family and its values so much more. It also made me realize that it's naïve to think that everyone experiences childhood that way. We rarely know what's going on inside families, and kids can be really good at hiding things when they're afraid.

I want kids to have a strong, supportive family like I did. I want them to experience unconditional love. I don't want them to be afraid of their parents. Our family is nearly always a core, defining part of who we become. Fortunately for me, I have a family that I can hold onto tightly, knowing that no matter what happens, I can count on them. Although much of this book is about letting go, my family is a part of me that I won't let go of.

I wish that were true for everyone.

CHAPTER 17
IT'S NOT FOREVER

The Mother's Day before we lost the house, I received a rolling briefcase for a gift. This was a great gift for me because I tend to have trouble with my shoulders, neck and back—in part because I'm lugging around heavy briefcases, bags and purses. (And wearing heels. I know—don't judge me.)

And then we moved—to a second floor condo. With no elevator. Suddenly, the wheeled briefcase became a problem to get up and down those stairs. And the steps were outside, unprotected from the weather, which meant that in the winter, they were sometimes even more treacherous.

For some reason, I was complaining about this (in a light-hearted way, I'm sure) to Curt. He just looked at me and breezily said, "It's not forever." That stopped me in my woe-is-me tracks. I knew, of course, that I wasn't going to live there forever, but at the time, feeling stuck as I was, it *felt* like forever. Once Curt reminded me that it wasn't, I was able to accept the fact that for *this year*, I wouldn't be able to use the bag. I could easily switch back to something else and not worry about it.

We sometimes make decisions as if they have to be permanent, as though we can't change those decisions if they don't work out, or if we change what we're doing in other ways.

Yesterday, I met with a coaching colleague of mine, and we were talking about a recent innovation she had made to her practice. She had added a monthly networking event that was more of a small discussion group. Each month was at a different location, with a different topic, and limited to about twelve women. It was only designed to last about an hour, so when she and I met, I asked if she had considered continuing the group discussions in a private online forum. She told me she had thought about it and then started to tell me the pros and cons of doing that. I listened while she enumerated each "side," and then told her of Curt's rather stinging lesson on pros and cons (though I was *much* gentler!).

He and I were in the car, driving to a meeting with one of his clients. I was talking to him about a client I had, and the decision I was trying to help her make. I started talking about the pros and cons of each option, when he nearly drove off the road in indignation. "Pros and cons?! Seriously?!" Apparently that wasn't the right answer.

"Pros and cons, *in isolation,* can often lead you to the very worst answer," he explained. "Instead, look at what you are trying to accomplish, and see which solution moves you closer to that end result," he finished. Put that way, it made complete sense, but I confess, his initial reaction made me squirm: remember—I'm the one who hates to be wrong. And I was *clearly* wrong here!

To my coaching friend, I suggested that, "instead of pros and cons in isolation, it might be better to ask what are you trying to achieve."

"Building relationships," she said simply. And then the light went on and she continued, "which means I should do that."

We laughed, and I joked, "See? Wasn't that easy?" I went on to suggest that it didn't have to be forever. One of her "cons" of adding a free online discussion forum was deciding what to do with it if she added a paid group coaching service. She might want to make the online discussion forum part of that package, instead of a free service provided to those who attended the networking event (for free).

I just smiled, channeled Curt and said, "The decision doesn't have to be forever. If you add a paid group coaching service and want to change the online discussion forum you can. Because what you're trying to achieve might be different, your decision might change as well."

Getting stuck in Foreverland means I'm often guilty of trying to see the whole staircase before I take the first step, but most of the time, that's not necessary or productive. My friend was trying to make a decision about a service she was considering *now,* based on what she *might* do in the future. Asking the question, "Will this move me closer to what I'm trying to achieve?" helps take down that compulsive insistence on seeing the whole staircase. If it moves me closer, it's probably a good thing to do.

Despite the fact that we *know* things are constantly changing, it's sometimes hard to see past where we are right now. It's a challenge to remember that, "This, too, shall pass." But remembering that something is not forever, and being able to visualize what the "after" looks like, can truly be a way to get us through the difficult times and keep us moving forward.

The week we were finally out of options on our house and I knew we were moving was one of the worst of my life. In that one-week period, I had to find a place to live, pack up the entire house, rent a truck and find people to help us move. It was emotionally devastating, and the shame in telling people what had happened was agonizing. One of the things that got me through it was to keep reminding myself that, "By Friday, this will all be over." I kept my eye on the light at the end of the tunnel—Saturday. I kept reminding myself that this week from hell was not forever.

Of course, in that situation, I knew when that tunnel would end. Other crises are not that clear cut, which makes it more difficult.

I became pregnant with our second child when we lived in Omaha. I was so excited! My first pregnancy with Kierra had gone smoothly, so I had no reason to believe this one might be different. But, unfortunately, in the first trimester, I suffered a miscarriage—on Labor Day no less. Oh, the sad irony. Watching the ultrasound tech look for any sign that my baby was still there, still alive was pure agony. When she had nothing but bad news to deliver, she left us alone in the room and told us to take our time.

I cried. And cried. And then I cried some more. Finally, we emerged to see that the nurse had waited outside the exam room the entire time in case we needed anything. Despite my grief, I felt guilty that we had made her wait for us, when I'm sure she was quite busy. But it was a kindness I've not forgotten.

People say ignorant things to you when you've had a miscarriage—painfully ignorant things. Their intentions are good, but they're just not thinking. One woman, in particular, said, "Well, you're young. You can have more kids." As though they are interchangeable.

A woman I worked with sent me a bouquet of flowers, but other than that, no one really acknowledged the loss. It's as though, because the child wasn't born, she doesn't actually exist, so what is there to grieve over? I'm sure there are many who will say they "forgot" that I had a miscarriage. They're not being deliberately cruel; it's just hard to remember someone that never drew a breath outside her mother's womb. But I still remember. And I still cry on occasion.

But that was only the beginning of hell week. When we returned home, I just couldn't bear to be cooped up in our two-bedroom apartment, so after lunch, we strapped Kierra into her car seat and went for a drive.

And the car broke down. I don't remember now precisely what the problem was, or even where we were, because my mind was obviously elsewhere. But I do know I didn't want to be stuck wherever we were any more than I wanted to be stuck in the apartment. We were finally able to fix whatever the issue was and head back home. I was exhausted at this point, physically and emotionally. Ah, but the day was young. There was more to come.

When we finally got back home, there was a note on the door from the *fire department*. Apparently, a hot coal had fallen out of the grill onto our deck and caused a small fire. Although there wasn't a lot of damage (and none in the apartment, thankfully), there was a pretty big mess on our deck and the deck of our downstairs neighbor. Firefighters with axes are more concerned about putting out the fire than being tidy, which is as it should be, of course.

But messy has different implications for different people, and the good times were still not over.

A few days later, emergency personnel were back at our complex, this time at our neighbor's garage. His wife had committed suicide. He told us his wife had suffered from OCD (Obsessive Compulsive Disorder) for years, engaging in such behaviors as combing the fringe on their rug and always wanting everything in its place at all times. He blamed her death on "our" fire, saying that the mess that had spilled over to their deck had pushed her over the edge.

The miscarriage.
The car trouble.
The fire.
The suicide.

All this had occurred in the span of a week, with three of the four events in the *same day*. I *never* want to have another week like that. It was just one blow after another. There was no known "end point" like with the house. After each thing happened, I would just hold my breath and wonder, "Is that it for a while? Are we done with the bad stuff for a while?" For me, it's the not knowing that can sometimes cause me the most trouble. It's hard to project past the hell-driven experiences when you don't know when you *will* be past.

I also never want to live in Omaha again. People try to balance things out by reminding me that it wasn't all bad; Logan was born there the following year. I look them square in the eye and tell them that yes, Logan was and is a wonderful blessing, *but,* if he had been born in Iowa, he would not have been breech. This usually causes people to throw up their hands and wave the white flag of surrender.

Joking aside, you would think that these experiences would have taught me quite clearly that bad times *do* pass, even if we don't know when that will happen. But it felt like there were so *many* bad things, and they often overlapped, that it was just one continuous onslaught of bad "luck."

Curt's comment that day about my briefcase was a reminder that nothing is forever. Let go of the bad things that happened, hold tight to the good, and keep moving forward.

CHAPTER 18
FINANCIAL ANOREXIA

One of the consistent questions I ask my mentor is, "How do you hear *God's* voice?" That's not the complete question, however, and usually gets followed up with two more: "How do you know if it is God's voice or your own?" and "How do you know it's God's plan versus what *you* want to do?" Like the time he was explaining a life insurance concept to me, I listened but didn't understand. I asked him to tell me again.

But recognizing the voice of God is a harder concept than borrowing from your life insurance contract. I listen again, and I read. And read. And think and pray. And sometimes I get close, and other times I feel even more confused than when I started. Occasionally, I stumble upon answers (or more questions) to other things I struggle to understand.

One such day, I was re-reading Bill Hybels' book about prayer, looking for answers. And I liked it until the very end, when he started talking about the severely under-resourced in the world. And suddenly, the only thing I could think of was, "I'm never good enough. I never give enough. There are still starving children in India (or Africa, or my own 'back yard.')." As if it's all up to me to solve that problem. It's as though, at a subconscious level, I feel like

I'm not allowed to have anything until all those people living in such abject poverty have enough to live on.

A bit later, I happened to come across a short video for *Simplify*, based upon Hybels' newest book of the same name, and apparently recorded at his home. And it's a *beautiful* home. Move-in ready, don't-change-a-thing, live-there-the-rest of-my-life beautiful (but not in a creepy, stalker way). It's not a mansion, but it is a beautiful, warm, welcoming home. And I'm confused. Here is a *pastor* who is talking about great need, yet he himself lives in a lovely home. His daughter drives a large SUV. He dresses well. I am missing something. I struggle to know what I'm "allowed" to have without feeling guilty.

—=+ +=—

Jim Rohn talks about a turning point in his life when he lied to a Girl Scout who was selling cookies. I don't remember the specific lie, but it was designed to cover up the fact that he didn't have even $2 to buy a box of cookies. It was a lie—and an epiphany—born out of shame.

My own "Girl Scout cookie" moment involved an injury to my shoulder. The first day, I loaded up on ibuprofen, so the pain was tolerable. But the *next* day, after sleeping on it all night, I reached above my head to wash my hair in the shower and nearly passed out from the pain. Literally—almost passed out, complete with silver "fish" swimming in my vision. I quickly realized I was not going to be able to pull a shirt on over my head; I would need to wear shirts that buttoned up front. So I went to my closet in search of a shirt that buttoned, only to discover nearly all my short-sleeved shirts pulled over my head. It then occurred to me that I did not have the money to just go buy a bunch of new shirts that *did* button up (and besides—how was I going to go buy new shirts when I couldn't put on a shirt to go shopping for the shirts I *could* put on?

Talk about a vicious cycle). It wasn't a moment of shame, per se. It was a moment of *How did I get here?*

I felt deprived. But again, that curiosity—how did I get here? Although I certainly wasn't wealthy in high school or college, I didn't feel *deprived*. I recalled a story I once read about boiling a frog. If you drop a frog in boiling water, he will immediately jump out. But if you put a frog in a pot of cool water and then gradually increase it until it's boiling, the frog will not jump out. The change is so subtle he doesn't realize what's happening until it's too late.

Although I've recently read that this story isn't true, it is still a good analogy for my life. I have cut back and cut back until I am living such a life of deprivation that I literally lost my house, have no money for clothes or even *fun*. I am slowly being boiled to death.

I blame this in part on the fact that not only am I a people pleaser, but also a God-pleaser. That seems like it would be a good thing, but in me, it results in getting all tied up in knots trying to figure out what I'm supposed to do. I want to do the right thing, and I hate making mistakes. Combining this aversion to error with my desire to always do the right thing in God's eyes creates a paralyzing fear of making an irrevocable mistake with God—I don't want to spend eternity in hell.

Yes, I know about forgiveness and grace, but in the back of my mind there is always this voice saying, "But what if you make a mistake that He *won't* forgive?" And that keeps me from taking *any* steps. Kind of like the guy in the Bible who buries his one talent so his master doesn't punish him for losing it in the stock market (ok, not the stock market, but you get my drift).

I think I know what I need to do to change my life, but I constantly second-guess myself—what if those changes aren't what *God* wants me to do? What if it's just me doing what *I* want?

Sometimes I think I read too much (although that passes quickly). Often I think too much (that doesn't pass as quickly).

What if I don't give money to that beggar? What if I don't go visit someone in the hospital (or prison)? What if I don't give enough money to the starving children in India, Africa or my own back yard? What if I'm not kind enough, generous enough or forgiving enough? What if I am not, simply, *enough*?

And then it plays out this way—if I am not good enough, then I don't deserve the good things in life. I don't deserve anything more than basic existence. And with that, I have my diagnosis.

I am a financial anorexic.

I have cut back farther and farther and farther until I've nearly killed myself financially. I lost my house. I have no real savings of my own, and I have no money for clothes or the fun things in life. Until recently, I drove a car with 190,000 miles and rust. And so it goes. Is that pious? Does living as though I'm at poverty level make me a better person? Less "greedy?"

The reason Bill Hybels' book bothers me is because it is about financial *obesity*, but obesity is not my problem. My story is about me depriving myself of reasonable and necessary financial "calories." Yet even though my head knows I'm financially starving, my heart continues to believe I have a weight problem.

It's like the physical anorexic—she looks in the mirror and sees a fat person, despite the bones jutting out through translucent skin. She knows that the number on the scale is alarmingly, life-threateningly low, yet her body image keeps her starving herself. Bill Hybels' book disturbs me because I feel like it's judging me as financially obese when in fact I have the opposite problem. And I wonder how much more I have to "lose" to be good enough.

Enough. ENOUGH. **ENOUGH!**

Earlier this year, I received a gift card to Barnes & Noble. One of the books I purchased was Max Lucado's book, *Grace*. And it was *such* a gift. So freeing, so forgiving, so full of the very grace he writes about. And then I bought Steve Harvey's book, *Act Like a Success, Think Like a Success*. In many respects, this motivational book by a comedian was very different from the faith book by a preaching minister and best-selling author. Yet in other ways, they were very much the same.

Both books spoke of second chances, of learning from mistakes, and about God's grace through it all. And a small seedling of hope—*true* hope, not the political kind we're always promised—began to grow in my soul. Maybe *I* could be forgiven, maybe *I* could be "enough," and maybe, just maybe *I* could be financially healthy. Me.

But first I had to let go of the idea that I wasn't good enough or that I didn't deserve to be financially healthy. I had to let go of my mother's belief that "other people" had money—not me. I had to stop listening to people who were constantly talking about people with money being greedy (usually this "conversation" came about right before the offering was collected), because that wasn't my problem. I had to constantly remind myself that if I was serving people, I would earn money and should *not* feel guilty about it, or feel like I had to give it all away. I had to stop undervaluing my work, discounting my fees and "donating" my writing and my speaking except for very specific reasons.

I had an interesting conversation with Curt one day about this very thing. I had been invited to speak at a half-day summit. I had set my speaking fees, and they had agreed to them, but with a new fiscal year, new officers were elected and a new person was assigned to work with me. She began making some noise about my fee being too high and perhaps withdrawing the invitation to speak.

I panicked a bit because I was counting on this income. Because this was an association (i.e., non-profit), and because I thought I might be able to get further work from it, I asked Curt if I should discount my fees so they didn't cancel. He just gave me one of those "Have I taught you nothing?" looks and said one word "No."

Then he went on to outline a brilliant strategy that I might suggest instead that would benefit everyone.

Ultimately, that offer was declined, but they still paid my full fee, and the former president apologized for the misunderstanding. Had I discounted my rate, I would have given the same presentation but been paid considerably less. To quote a classic Curt question: "Why would I do that?" The only reason I was considering the discount was fear—fear that if I didn't, they might withdraw their offer. It had nothing to do with the value of my work.

⟞⟝ ⟞⟝

I went back to one of my prayer journals recently, and on one of the pages where I recorded the thoughts I had during my quiet prayer time, I found a place where I was considering the concept of "bucket filling" from Tom Rath and Donald Clifton's book, *How Full is Your Bucket?* The premise/question of the book is whether people fill your bucket or take from it. But it occurred to me that while it is nice when others fill my bucket with positive interactions, it is ultimately up to me to fill my own bucket. Others are not responsible for my happiness—I am. But when I looked at my metaphorical bucked, I realized that it was full all right—full of *sludge*. How could I empty that sludge, and then fill it with clean, sparkling water? And then I read this in my prayer journal:

"Stop depriving yourself! Fill your bucket and don't feel guilty about it!"

It was so powerful, and so contrary to my mindset at this time that I knew it was God speaking to me. *He* wasn't depriving me, *I* was. And here was the answer to two things I was struggling with: how to hear God's voice in my everyday life, and how to get past this bent toward financial anorexia.

I became more able to hear God's voice when I actually took time everyday to *listen* for it. While that sounds obvious, I had never before set aside a specific time each day for prayer. I prayed, of course, when I was having a problem, and I was pretty good about saying "thank you" for things, but in terms of a specific time every day, one that was not prompted by anything but the need to meet with God? No. I had to turn down the noise from both the exterior world and the internal chatter.

Writing down my thoughts everyday made it easier to discern what God was trying to tell me versus my own ideas. I discovered that the more consistent I was in reserving time to listen, the more I heard. I was better able to *recognize* God's voice, just as we are more able to recognize the voice of *people* with whom we speak regularly. And—writing everything down helped me not lose it. Sometimes, when I went back and read my thoughts, they were more meaningful than when I originally wrote them.

With regard to the financial anorexia, I did something that was very difficult for me. I started spending some money on myself, on things that made me happy, rather than things I thought I *should* spend it on.

I got my piano tuned, and beyond the absolute joy of playing a piano that's in tune, I got to hear some beautiful, original music the piano tuner had written. I bought a sewing machine so I can create some beautiful things for my home. And when I told my friend in Cedar Rapids—who is a *wonderfully* talented seamstress, quilter and knitter—she offered to teach me how to quilt! A new legacy gift I can make for my family, perhaps. I even bought some new clothes (although as I think about it, I *still* didn't buy any shirts that button up the front!). I have a new-to-me car that has low miles and no rust and is a pleasure to drive. I'm beginning to slowly put money away.

And, most important for me, I have focused on the *blessing* of all of this—not guilt over having something that someone else might not have. I let go of the questions about worth and whether or not I deserve them. I have simply accepted those things with gratitude and enjoyed them. The end of Hybels' other book, *Simplify,* says this: "The Christian faith is not fundamentally against material blessings. Although we shouldn't put our *hope* in wealth, God gives us good things, and He wants us to enjoy them...I make no apologies for walking with God and enjoying his bounty."

That's a much healthier attitude. I hear You, God.

CHAPTER 19

VICTIMHOOD

When my dad died, I was only 12 years old, which meant I got a lot of attention. People felt sorry for me (who wouldn't?), and my Aunt Marilyn, in her loving attempt to perhaps distract me, took me shopping for a dress. I don't really remember *why* we were shopping, although perhaps that's when my mom went to the funeral home to make arrangements for the service, and she needed a place for us to go (although I don't recall that my brother was with us). I'm sure there were many things about that time that I was unaware of, given my age.

In any event, as soon as I saw the dress, I knew I wanted it. In my 12-year-old mind, it was perfect. It was a yellow floor-length dress with flowers on it. At that age, I was the proverbial ugly duckling; braces, glasses—the whole nine yards of awkward pre-adolescence. But in that dress, I felt beautiful.

Of course, at that age, I didn't know it was totally inappropriate for a funeral; I just wanted it because I wanted to look beautiful for my dad's service. Aunt Marilyn, who didn't have the heart to refuse me much of anything that day, bought it for me, but I didn't get to wear it to the funeral. Instead, I wore an "appropriate" navy blue, knee-length dress.

I suppose she bought me the dress because I wanted it and she wanted to somehow do something that would ease my suffering, but I'm sure she knew I would not be wearing it to the funeral. I stuffed the yellow dress in the back of my closet and never wore it. When I finally outgrew it, I simply threw it away. I pretended it didn't matter, but there was a part of me that was angry at not being allowed to wear it to the funeral. I suppose there was another part of me that was humiliated at being so "wrong" about what was appropriate—I did not (nor do I still) like being wrong.

While I understand that we want to support people who are grieving, especially little people, one of the lessons I subconsciously picked up was that when you are suffering, people are nice to you and you get attention. This, in turn, causes us to play the victim card, which can eventually lead to fatigue for the people around us, if it's played too often.

The niece of a friend of mine was killed in a car accident just a few days after Christmas in 2014. She and her fiancé were traveling on a backcountry road following a party. Ironically, she was driving because her fiancé had been drinking—they were being responsible and *safe*. But black ice does not care about that, and she spun out, crossed the center line and was hit broadside by a pick up truck, killing her instantly. Her fiancé suffered only minor injuries and was released from the hospital shortly thereafter.

Her death was tragic for the very reason that a young person's death is always tragic—so much unrealized potential. She was just getting ready to start graduate school, she was going to be married, and she had been active in so many things in college. She had so much to give, and so much to experience, but it was all gone in a moment.

I remember when Logan was in elementary school. He and Randy and I went to Ledges State Park. There are lots of trails to hike, but there was one that led to a cliff high above a stream. Logan, fearless as he is, stepped right up to the edge to peer over.

There was no guardrail to protect him from falling, and in that moment, I felt a terror like never before (or since). Although he has great balance, there is always the possibility of an unstable rock. He would not survive a fall from that distance. Although I wanted to yell, "Logan! Get back!" I was afraid I might startle him and cause him to fall. All I could do was stand there, paralyzed by what might happen, and wait for him to step back of his own accord.

We never went there with him again. I just could not risk losing him. And even though I experienced the sheer terror at the *possibility* of losing my child, I still cannot imagine how it would feel to *actually* have my child die. My experience had a happy ending. But for my friend's family, the ending was not happy. Their daughter did not come back safely.

Everyone understandably rallied around the family to comfort and support them. Several months later, the college this young woman had attended (and where she had competed in track) had a track meet where they specifically honored her. The college was a few hours away, and my friend and her family did not attend. Not because they didn't love this young woman or her family, but because they had issues of their own. My friend had just had been diagnosed with melanoma and had undergone outpatient surgery to remove the cancerous cells. Her husband had just lost his job. Their daughter was still dealing with issues from back surgery. Despite all this, her sister-in-law was angry with her. She felt they should have been there, and she made that clear in rather "subtle" ways, commenting on how nice the turnout was, how caring the people were and so forth. The implication, of course, was that my friend should have been there.

I am not expressing an opinion as to whether they should have been there, or how long is an "appropriate" time to grieve, or anything other than this: When we get stuck in victimhood, everything becomes all about us. We forget that others are dealing with their own struggles. We forget that support is supposed to help us get through the initial shock and tragedy, not be a permanent status. We shouldn't expect casseroles, yellow dresses and mandatory attendance at special events for the rest of our lives—they are *temporary.*

An extreme example of using victim status as a way to get attention (and, in this case, money) showed up in the news this year. An Iowa woman claimed her daughter was dying of cancer, going so far as to inject drugs (cannabis oil) and insert a feeding tube into her daughter, shave her daughter's head and create a bucket list for the little girl. Numerous fundraisers were held, collecting upwards of $25,000. The problem with collecting money to help offset the costs of a catastrophic health diagnosis? Her daughter didn't *have* cancer. She was a perfectly healthy little girl. Victim status was *manufactured* by mom and rewarded by the unsuspecting community. Many, many people were hurt by her fabrications.

But most of the time, victim status only hurts *us.* We've learned that being a victim draws sympathy and kindness, so we look for more ways to be victims, or to exploit previous victim-status. But ultimately, being a victim means we stay stuck in whatever is causing us pain. We can't move forward, because that requires giving up victimhood. We don't seem to understand that we would be happier if we *did* move out of victim status, take control of our actions and overcome those struggles.

My friend Megan is having a challenging time at work. Let me say right up front that I believe her when she says they are mistreating her. But here's where it gets to be a problem: everyone has so strongly empathized with her, she hardly knows how to behave as other than a victim of her work environment.

When she makes a thinly veiled complaint on Facebook, the comments of support pour in, generally telling her that she is a wonderful person and her boss is, well, let's just say *less* than wonderful. She receives encouraging notes and even small gifts—flowers, sweets and wine—to help her "get through it." Again—I don't doubt that her work environment is a struggle, and I'm all for supporting people in difficult situations.

But.

I think we need to ask ourselves whether our actions are actually helping or hindering. Megan has been dealing with this for a number of *years*. Initially, I started out like everyone else, offering the "traditional" support and encouragement. But in the last few months, I have moved to asking questions to try to help her see options so that she can regain control of her decisions about her job.

But her responses to every suggestion are things like, "They would never do that." Or, "That's impossible." It's as though she's so afraid to leave her victim status that she refuses to even try something that might alleviate the pain. She has given up all control over her situation in order to receive the "perks" of being a victim.

The situation reached a turning point for me a few months ago. There was a thing going around Facebook that asked you to list three things for which you were grateful, for five consecutive days, and then to "tag" five other people to do the same. I specifically sent this to a few people I knew were struggling, hoping they would be reminded of the good things in their life rather than the things that weren't working. Most of them responded with gratitude for the things that were important to them—family and friends, employment and good health—but not Megan. Megan said, "I don't have three things for which to be grateful for one day, let alone five."

My first thought was, "*Wow.*" It was like the meeting you have at work about a new project. Everyone's excited about it, and then there's that *one person* who insists on completely bursting the bubble, sucking out all the positive energy and replacing it with a big batch of black "negativity."

I was pretty sure *I* could *easily* think of many things for which Megan could be grateful. It felt like she was deliberately ignoring all the things that were going well in her life and focusing instead on the one thing that wasn't working—her job. But she wasn't willing to do anything to change it. She was stuck—big time—and she apparently intended to live in stuck for as long as she could.

Why? Why do we do that?

I'm not a psychologist, and I don't pretend to know what motivates other people (although I can sometimes make a pretty good guess). However, having been in a similar situation as Megan, I can tell you why *I* did it (although I could not have articulated, or admitted this when I was in the middle of it). First, it became a learned helplessness. When your boss crushes every idea you present, you quit presenting new ideas. When he insists on micromanaging your every move and decision, you lose confidence in your ability to make good decisions. When your attempts to do great work are thwarted at every turn of the road, you give up. I get it. Believe me, I am painfully aware of how that works and feels.

However, *changing* the situation required me to acknowledge and admit *my* role in the dysfunction. I didn't have a (difficult) conversation with my boss about how I felt. Instead, I began to complain about him behind his back, to whoever would listen—*and* commiserate. I quit but stayed (though not for long—after only a year, I quit and left). I forgot to apply my cardinal rule for others to myself—I will let you complain about it for a bit, but then I expect you to do something to try and fix it. If you don't, I don't want to hear any more complaining. Instead, I decided it was easier to complain about it rather than do the work necessary to *fix* it.

The reason victim *status* is so poisonous if allowed to continue is that we think it gives us permission to behave badly, thinking everyone will forgive us because of what we're going through. We can't be held responsible for our behavior because we are under such *stress*. And we think that other people will continue to respond with sympathy and concern. But the drama gets old, and eventually people either start to avoid us or they become impatient enough with our behavior to call us out on it.

Although I don't avoid my friend, I certainly do not ask her how work is going. And if she brings it up, I try to steer the conversation in a different direction. If she insists on talking about it, I often find a way to end the conversation. Initially I told myself I just couldn't do the drama anymore. But in truth, I simply didn't *want* to do the drama. So I decided to let her go until she lets go of her own drama and victim status. If and when she chooses to not hold herself and others hostage to her plight, I will be first in line to support her in *that* endeavor.

People still respond with empathy and concern when I tell them my dad died when I was young. But I'm working hard to not let myself use that concern as permission to drop back into victim status. Yes, it was tragic. Yes, it shaped who I am today in many different ways, both good and bad. But I can acknowledge all that *and* let go of my identity as a victim. It's healthier for me, and for others around me.

CHAPTER 20
GIVING

There's nothing like an editor to point out your propensity for whining in certain chapters. Kindly and gently, of course, but also honestly. It's one of the things I most appreciate—her willingness to tell me the truth so that I can do my best writing. The whiny chapters end up being re-writes with a *lot* of cutting (and very little pasting). Of course, a really good editor will also tell you when something you've written doesn't resonate for some reason, or is confusing. The ones that are confusing are generally easy fixes—because I'm so "close" to the story, it doesn't occur to me that others might not understand what I'm describing. A few more details, and it's good to go.

Other times, though, my internal response reminds me more of that classic parenting question—*What part of "no" do you not understand?* In other words, what I'm trying to convey seems so obvious to me that I'm not sure why she doesn't "get it." One such story I ended up cutting all together, because I realized there was just too big of a "back story" for it to make sense (and the former boyfriend who was the subject of said chapter will probably be glad he's not "featured"). But the other one, the one that lacked the "emotional overtones" of the other chapters was harder to fix.

Many of the chapters of this book have dealt with letting go of attitudes, beliefs or relationships. The chapters that have dealt with letting go of actual things have generally been things that I have not *willingly* let go of—like my house. This was obviously a highly emotional event, and it's easy to feel the pain of it even if you haven't experienced foreclosure yourself. It's a *big* event that most people can understand. But the $3 that is the subject of the story I'm about to tell? A bit harder to convey its impact unless you've been there.

This chapter *is* a bit different. Although it's about money, it's about money in the context of giving, rather than simply letting go. Letting go signifies a passive (or sometimes resistant) attitude. Giving, on the other hand, is an affirmative thing—you don't just *let* it happen, you *make* it happen.

So here's the story. And if it *doesn't* resonate with you, maybe that's a good thing. Maybe that means you haven't experienced scarcity at this level.

I went to a restaurant on the other side of town to meet some friends for dinner. I ordered a half salad, but later, when looking at the bill more carefully, realized I had been charged for a full salad. Yes, I know, the price difference between the two is small. But there *is* a difference, and research shows that someone who has experienced scarcity on a rather consistent level will notice *and* follow up (good to know I'm predictable).

What I didn't know was whether I had *received* a full salad. After a phone call with the manager, it turned out that I got what I paid for, but, as he pointed out, I did not get what I *ordered*. As a way to make it right, he generously offered to send me a gift card that could be used at any of their four locations. The gift card was for $25—which was significantly more than the cost of the salad. It was a very good customer service experience. He listened, he apologized, he made it right.

A few days after receiving the card, I decided to treat myself to a meal out. I asked my server ahead of time if I could include his tip on the card (because I've been caught short-cashed in situations where you *can't* put the tip on the gift card), and he said that I could. When my bill came, the amount plus a 19% tip, rounded up to the nearest dollar came to around $22 (I know—it's kind of a weird method, but it works for me most of the time).

I sat and thought about that total for a minute. If I left an "appropriate" tip, I would have $3 left on the card, which wouldn't go far enough on a subsequent visit to make any real difference. On the other hand, although an extra $3 wasn't a lot in terms of dollars, it was a *huge* tip in terms of percentage. I decided to leave the whole thing.

And I get it—it's *$3*—not something people typically ruminate over. But because I had been living in the land of "not enough" for so long, it was a big deal to leave the entire thing as a tip—even though the amount was small.

In their book *Scarcity,* authors Sendhil Mullainathan and Eldar Shafir note that those who live in financial scarcity are *very* focused on how much things cost—they are "experts" who are less likely to be overcharged because they are tracking so carefully (which probably explains why I called the manager in the first place).

That's why leaving the full $3, small as it was, was such a big deal for me. Scarcity deemed me not only an "expert," but also taught me to hold on tightly to every dollar. Leaving $3 was not about "letting go" of that money. It was about a more intentional *giving* of that $3. For me, this was an opportunity to be generous, which is a blessing that those of us caught in scarcity don't often experience. It was significant, too, because it reflected a shift in my attitude. Maybe *I* could be generous, even if that generosity was small to start with.

In the classic book *A Tree Grows in Brooklyn,* there is a line about coffee that I have always found intriguing. The mother says: "Francie [her daughter] is entitled to one cup each meal like the rest. If it makes her feel better to throw it way rather than to drink it, all right. I think it's good that people like us can waste something once in a while *and get the feeling of how it would be have lots of money and not have to worry about scrounging."* (Emphasis mine.)

That's the way I felt about that $3—it gave me the feeling of being generous, without worrying about hanging on to every last dollar.

Of course, like many people, I told myself that when I had more, I would give more. But according to a Harvard study, that's backward. When we *give* more, we *receive* more. Although counterintuitive, the giving comes *first.* The research demonstrated that, on average, for every dollar donated to charity, the giver receives back $3.75.

The faith–based person that I am is geeking out over this scientific support of the Biblical principle of tithing. But if you aren't a person of faith, the secular research, in a nutshell, goes something like this: Giving makes you feel good, and when you feel good, you're more likely to be successful. Giving helps relieve stress, which means you're more productive when you give. And, interestingly, people who give more are perceived to be leaders, which leads to the almost inevitable conclusion that they will likely be more successful.

When I read about the Harvard study, I initially thought that I must be an anomaly, because I wasn't getting that $3.75 ROI. But if I'm honest, I think that what was really going on was that when I gave, I gave fearfully and out of obligation. I *physically* gave, but *mentally* hung onto the money. I didn't want to be guilted into giving, either, even if it's for a "good cause." And I especially don't like it when a minister tells me to "let go of" my "stuff" at offering time.

In fact, I'm just defiant enough to *reduce* my giving when I feel like I'm being compelled to give.

I know. Probably not what Jesus would do.

The point is, I wasn't really giving; I was just letting go of my money. Big difference.

So I decided to test the Harvard theory, but this time to *really* test it. I was going to give, and give *joyfully,* and with gratitude, even if it was a small amount. Not out of fear. Not out of obligation. I sat down right then and there and wrote a check to a local mission-based service organization. I blessed the money as I sent it on its way, expressing gratitude that I was able to give, even though it was only $25. I assumed that no gift was too small to be helpful.

A few weeks after I gave the $25, I received the gift of a book from a friend. And then I received a phone call from an insurance broker telling me that there was a commission check for me, but the organization needed my current mailing address. Those two things didn't quite add up to the $3.75 ROI the Harvard research discovered, but it was a start.

☰⊹ ⊹☰

In my experience, when I give out of a place of love and joy, I can't out-give God. Heck, I'm not sure I can even out-give my son.

Logan is an ultimate giver. As a child, he had a beloved teddy bear named White Bear. White Bear was, as you've probably guessed, white, but he was the softest, cuddliest teddy bear I've ever seen. He was the perfect size for a toddler, and he went everywhere with Logan. One day at daycare, another child, probably about 18 months old, was crying because he didn't want his mother to leave him. Logan quietly observed the little boy's distress, and then walked over and simply handed White Bear to him to comfort him. The mom and the daycare provider nearly cried.

Such a simple act, yet so intuitive and so generous, especially from one so small.

When he was in high school, Logan noticed a homeless man standing with his dog at a busy intersection in front of Target. Logan went in and bought the man food and a gallon of water, and also bought dog food for the man's dog. When I asked him what prompted the dog food purchase, he explained that if he didn't buy dog food, the man would probably share *his* food with the dog. He wanted the man to be able to eat everything he gave him, without worrying about feeding his dog.

Keep in mind that Logan did not receive an allowance at this point. He had a job, and his job provided his spending money. But he didn't worry about it or overanalyze it. He saw someone who needed food, and he bought him some food.

As a reward for his routine giving, Logan regularly receives money in rather odd ways. He once bought a pair of pants that were on clearance at a sporting goods store. The pants had been returned because they had a small hole in them, but since Logan was planning to wear them hiking in the mountains, he didn't care. He paid $7 for them. When he got them home, he discovered a $10 bill in the pocket!

In December, he was in a motorcycle wreck. Initially, he related his experience in his own unique fashion. "One minute I was riding down the street, and the next I was watching my bike slide away from me." More details revealed that he and his bike were not just sliding, but were sliding *into an intersection*. A man in the car next to him saw this as it was happening and sped up into the intersection to stop traffic, and then watched in total amazement as Logan slid, rolled and popped up on his feet.

That mind/body kinesthetic thing may not be an advantage in school, but it can save your life.

But here's the money connection. The bike was totaled, and the insurance company wrote him a check for the Kelly Blue Book value of the motorcycle and accessories that were damaged. But because he had initially paid *less* than KBB for it, he actually *made money* on the wreck.

Now, I don't advocate getting in accidents as a way to make money. But because Logan is a giver, he is also a receiver, even under unique and sometimes bizarre situations. Giving money is quite different from letting it go, but for me, I have to first let go of the *attachment* to that money. Otherwise, I can't ever fully give it.

And that's why the $3 was so important. I let go of the *need* to hang on to it in order to give it freely. Because, according to Harvard, if I can't give it, I can't receive it, and I will place myself in a never-ending loop of scarcity.

That's not happening.

CHAPTER 21

PLANS AND PEOPLE

The common theme running throughout this book is, obviously, the idea of letting go. I didn't realize what a pattern this was until I started writing. Interestingly, if I had tried to outline the book (as is my natural inclination) instead of just *writing*, I might have missed that discovery. To paraphrase Abby from the hit TV show *NCIS*, "Don't plan; just go." Because when you plan, there's only one right answer. If you just go without any preconceived ideas of what you're looking for, you will "find along the way."

I should note, in case you haven't already figured it out, that this concept of "don't plan, just go" is *not* in my comfort zone.

This past weekend, my son and his girlfriend flew into Des Moines for a wedding that was taking place in North Liberty, a small town about 2½ hours east and a bit north of Des Moines. Originally, we were to pick them up on Friday evening and drive them to North Liberty. Then the plan changed, and we were to instead pick them up on Sunday and bring them back to Des Moines so that they could catch their flight out on Monday evening. Fine. I was playing for my choirs in church on Sunday, but we could leave after the 9 o'clock service and be in North Liberty around 12:30 for a late lunch before heading back home.

Then Randy suggested we try to have lunch with his oldest son Josh (and *his* daughter Aurora), in Cedar Rapids that same day (Cedar Rapids is about 20 minutes north of North Liberty). Josh agreed, and Logan was definitely on board. Saturday night, though, Josh let us know that his daughter had a Girl Scout meeting on Sunday that he needed to take her to. He wasn't sure of the time, but thought it was either 1:00 or 1:30.

Can you hear me beginning to sigh?

Randy decided that instead of having lunch with Josh and Aurora, we would just meet for ice cream when she was done at 3:00. I'm now beginning to grind my teeth, because that means we will get back to Des Moines considerably later than I had planned. But—the Cubs were on the radio at 3:00, so we could listen to them on the way home, and all would be fine.

We picked up Logan and his girlfriend, Aleyna, and then made another "since we're in Eastern Iowa anyway" stop at the apartment of friends of Kierra's. They live in a secure apartment building, so when we arrived, I called them to tell them we were there. Their car was in the parking lot, but there was no answer.

Take a deep breath.

Decisions about where to go for lunch (back in Iowa City) were difficult, and the first restaurant had a 30-minute wait. It started to rain. We landed at a sandwich shop full of giggling college kids and no empty tables for four. Finally, a table opened up and we were able to eat—and run. We dashed through the rain, piled into the car and headed back to Cedar Rapids, only to discover that the address Josh gave us for the ice cream place was wrong. Apparently it actually *does* make a difference to MapQuest if you put in Third Street *SW* rather than Third Street *SE*.

At that point, I gave up. I closed my eyes, took yet another deep breath and decided that I was just going to have to live with the fact that there *is no plan*. I can fume about it, or I can simply let it go and just drift right along with them, hoping that at *some point* we will actually get back home.

And of course, we did, but not without a lot of stress on my part. Thank heavens there was a bookstore to escape to while waiting to meet Josh at the ice cream and popcorn store. As an aside, I should mention that I had some of the best salted-caramel popcorn *ever* at this little shop.

But I am making progress. In the past, I would have let this stumbling, no-plan journey completely undo me, robbing me of that simple popcorn pleasure. But this time, I made the *decision* to not do that to myself.

But this chapter really isn't about planning or even letting go of my preconceived ideas of how things ought to go. It's about some of the things I discovered when I opened up to the insights that revealed themselves when I simply wrote instead of planning my writing down to that last little outlined detail.

Putting my thoughts and feelings into writing helped clarify what the stumbling blocks were, as well as the lessons I needed to learn in order to change and grow. It also helped me realize that, as hard as it can be to let go of things, and even beliefs, it can sometimes be even harder to let go of *people*, because we don't want to hurt them.

As difficult and painful as it was to let go of the house, the *house* didn't care who owned it. But people—people *do* care about being "let go." Now, admittedly, some are easier to let go of than others. This I discovered in the course of my coffee shop adventures.

Business philosopher Jim Rohn once observed that you are the sum of the five people you spend the most time with. I'm self-employed, and a self-employed *writer* no less, which means I often spend big chunks of my day alone. And as an introvert, I'm okay with that. But it puts a little different spin on Rohn's question. Instead of trying to think about whom I spent the *most* time with, I began thinking about the people with whom I was *starting* my day.

Several years ago, when I was working at the job from Hades, I began treating myself to a morning at a West Des Moines coffee shop every Saturday. During this "me time," I would read, write—whatever I wanted to do. There was a small gang of "regulars" that consisted of a couple of businessmen and a couple of lawyers, most of whom were retired or semi-retired. Simply by being a "regular" myself, I got to know them. But I found that I did not like all the political discussions, especially because one of the lawyers was a criminal defense attorney who always felt he had to be "on" and win every argument. He liberally sprinkled his conversation with insults, name-calling and the F-bomb, shouting down anyone who disagreed with him. I sat in a corner and put in my headphones, blocking out most of the conversation. And they generally left around 9 o'clock, so if I could just hold out until then, things would quiet down.

After I left that soul-sucking job and opened my own business, I began going to the coffee shop on an almost daily basis. It became my "office," offering a relatively comfortable place to sit and write, plus good coffee and free Wi-Fi. A cup of coffee was pretty cheap rent. But it turned out that the armchair politicians went every day, too, which made it a bit challenging that first hour. There were some days where that cup of coffee seemed hugely overpriced, given the nonsense I had to listen to in exchange.

When I read Rohn's comment, I realized that although I didn't spend the *most* time with those characters, I was starting my day with them, and that was not good. I switched locations (same great coffee, but without the caffeinated *discourse*), and found myself much more productive. It was an easy change, an easy "let go" of the people who were so loudly opinionated (To be fair, I should note that once the defense lawyer left the group, it was much quieter, and much more civil).

But what about friends?

Steve Harvey, comedian and author of the book *Act Like a Success, Think Like a Success*, notes, "[E]veryone who comes with you cannot go with you." And while my head recognizes the truth of that statement, my heart is a bit slower to catch up. It's painful to have people you care about willingly walk out of your life. It's hard not to chase after them, pleading with them to return. But neither chasing nor catching is the same as restoring.

People don't grow at the same rate, either; sometimes you can't keep pulling people along with you. If they can't (or won't) go willingly, it's time to let go. And sometimes people have life experiences that simply prevent them from continuing to journey with you. But the longer the relationship, the harder it can be to let go.

A few years back, I began feeling concerned over one particular friend named Lisa. We had been friends for years—ever since high school. We had been in each other's weddings, hosted baby showers for each other, supported each other through our mothers' deaths, and everything in between. We had *history*! But she and I were becoming increasingly negative. It was easy to commiserate over things that were not going well, over real and perceived slights, and people just not doing the "right" thing, much to our mutual aggravation. Pretty soon, our joint pity parties were leading us into a "celebration" of all that was wrong in our lives. But the negativity wasn't my only concern.

In 2002, a friend of mine committed suicide. She had exhibited many of the same behaviors prior to her suicide that I was seeing in Lisa now. It wasn't that I thought Lisa was suicidal—I didn't, but I did not want it to get to that point. I wanted to, as my mother used to say, "nip it in the bud," before it *did* get to that point.

Lisa tried to please everyone all the time while "simmering" inside. People close to her hurt her, and she never called them out on it. Instead, she kept that hurt bottled up inside and smiled on the outside. I wanted better for my friend. I wanted her to stand up for herself and take good care of *her*, rather than always putting everyone else first.

At one point, I became particularly concerned, and I finally decided to send her an email expressing that concern. Before you roll your eyes and say, *"Email? Really?"* you should know that I had tried to meet with her face-to-face, but although she had originally agreed, she ultimately canceled, saying she wasn't "feeling well."

Unwilling to stay silent, and afraid of what might happen if I did nothing, I spent an entire afternoon crafting the email, wanting to make sure it was worded just right—caring and compassionate but straightforward. I wanted her to know how much I cared about her, and that I wanted her to value herself the way I did. I believe a true friend is one who will always tell you the truth, but in a compassionate way. I believed she would know my intentions were good; I wanted the absolute best for her.

Apparently she either didn't agree or didn't read it the way I intended. She was angry and hurt, and she told me that I was "just another person" trying to tell her how to live her life. She assured me she had a *great* life and ultimately cut off our friendship. Of course, the fact that I was "another person" suggested that others were also concerned—it wasn't just me. And her "great life" had its own cracks, which became apparent the following year. But that is her story to tell, not mine.

I was crushed that I had been so misunderstood. I twice apologized for hurting her. I checked in a few weeks later but was again told that she was still "angry and hurt." So, I—let it go. And I was oddly at peace with this at the time. It was her decision to end the friendship, and I couldn't force her to forgive me and be friends again. I had been very afraid for her, and if I had not told her of my concerns and something had happened, I would not have been able to forgive myself.

And I realized that I felt lighter. Her negativity had never been about me (nor was mine about her), but I didn't realize that just participating in it and adding my own toxic measure every week was not healthy—for either of us. I certainly empathized with her, but I wanted her to stand up for herself and not let people treat her that way. I wanted her to set boundaries at work and with certain members of her family. I wanted to focus on and expand the good things that were going on, rather than the challenges.

But that's what *I* wanted.

I could point out what I was seeing, as well as why those things were concerning to me. I could phrase it as lovingly and as gently as I knew how, while still telling the truth. But ultimately, it was up to her as to how she would "hear" my words. It was up to her whether she wanted to make any changes, and it was up to her to decide whether to end our friendship.

As I write this, the question occurs to me—*Why was a 30-year friendship easier to let go of than a house?* I think it was easier because I believed I was making the right decision in sharing my concerns (even if she didn't agree). I had control over that decision, and I wasn't trying to take responsibility for *her* decisions. With the house, on the other hand, I refused to believe it was the right decision to let it go. I kept fighting and fighting to keep it, until it was forcibly removed from me and I lost any control over the decision.

⚊⧻ ⧻⚊

Letting go is clearly easier when *I* make the decision to let go, instead of someone else "making me" let go. But despite my self-congratulatory statements, there was another lesson to learn. Sometimes letting go isn't a one-time deal—it's a process. We let go and then we change our minds. We give it up and then want it back. It *doesn't* come back to us willingly, so we chase it down and *bring* it back.

Despite my assertion that I felt good about letting Lisa go, I continued to check in with her periodically. I'm not really sure why. Maybe I couldn't believe that 30 years of friendship were destroyed by a single email. Maybe I couldn't believe she would so easily write me off. Or perhaps it was my need-to-know personality ("Why would she do this?"), or my need to be *right* (not about her life, but about my intentions around my "intervention"). I didn't push, though, just asked how she was. Initially, the responses were a clipped, "I'm fine," despite the fact that I knew she was *not* fine. Those two words fairly bristled with righteous anger.

And then one day, I took a deep breath and emailed her, telling her I was going to be in her town and asking if she would like to meet. To my great surprise, she agreed and suggested we meet at a local restaurant after she was done working. I arrived first. When Lisa arrived, she didn't even sit down before she was asking small-talk questions. You know, the kind you ask when you're past the "I-just-met-you stage," but not quite to the "we've-been-friends-for-ages" stage.

Clearly *she* was going to set the tone for this first meeting. Because I was trying to repair this relationship without knowing what, specifically, had *caused* the rift, I let her control the direction of the conversation.

It was all very civil, but it was also as if there had been no break in our friendship—and I don't mean that in a good way. We have never spoken of that time, and so it feels unfinished. I reread the email I sent to her, and still I had no idea what I said that triggered her decision to kick me to the curb. I walk on eggshells around her, and we pretend nothing happened. But it's the proverbial elephant in the room, and that elephant is *not* getting smaller as time goes by. It blocks our ability to truly forgive and move past what happened because we don't talk about it. Oh, we do the socially correct things. And we speak and it *sounds* like things are fine again, but it doesn't *feel* that way to me.

And still I have hung on. This past year, I have reached out to her several times, suggesting that when she is in town, we get together. Those requests never get a response. It has been *four years* since the original email, and I feel like I am *still* "begging" for her forgiveness. It feels like she is still punishing me. And so I finally, bravely, said to myself—*I'm not going to do that anymore.* I realized I was getting angry. I was tired of trying, over and over, to repair the relationship only to have her "forgive" me on the surface, but continue to punish me.

I was angry that she trusted and valued our friendship so little that she was willing to end it over a single email that she perceived as hurtful, despite my best intentions. I realized she didn't really *want* to forgive me. She didn't want to talk about the email or what she thought I had done wrong, which was really the only way to really clear the air and move forward.

But there is a shift, too, in how I think about our relationship. It's no longer in the "bury the cat" category of letting go that Curt talks about; it's not an either/or proposition of letting go *or* hanging on. I don't have to assertively let her go. I can instead hold that relationship loosely. I am not chasing the friendship anymore, but neither am I forcing her out of my life.

If she chooses to stay and work with me to rebuild the relationship, great. If she chooses not to, then that friendship will just naturally fall through my fingers. All indications are that she is choosing that latter path. And that's her decision. *My* decision is that I'm going to move my attention, time and effort to people who *want* to be friends with me, and who want to invest *their* attention, time and effort into our friendship as well.

Ultimately, I have to let go of my insistence that things turn out the way *I* want or intend. People get to make their own decisions, and sometimes their decisions aren't going to be the same as mine. That's okay. They get to live their life.

And I get to live mine.

CHAPTER 22

CHILDHOOD FRIENDS

Facebook can sometimes be a wonderful thing. Yesterday, as I was re-writing a chapter about my best friend in sixth grade, I wondered again where she was. Her name was Stacey Gilbert, and she was a talented musician, sitting first chair in the flute (and piccolo) section. She was smart, and she was a talented artist. I attended church on the east side of Des Moines, but that was a bit of a haul to travel back and forth multiple times in a week, so I attended youth group with Stacey at the Presbyterian church in Johnston. We likely would have remained friends for many years.

Unfortunately (well, unfortunately for *me* anyway), her dad got a job transfer that moved the family out of state. In a time before texts, Instagram and Facebook, it was hard to maintain a long-distance friendship, and we gradually grew apart. The last I knew, she was married and living in Ohio, but I couldn't even remember her married name. I had looked for her on Facebook, but with no success. *Try one more time,* I thought. Since the chapter wasn't coming together the way I wanted it to, I decided a little procrastination was in order. I opened Facebook, typed in "Stacey Gilbert" and "Ohio" and hit enter.

And I found her. I *found* her!

I would recognize those dark, sparkling eyes and that bright smile anywhere. I sent her a message asking if she had gone to Johnston Community Schools when she was younger and if she had siblings named Shelly and Ryan, just to make sure. But as I scrolled through her list of friends, I *was* sure. Excitedly, I sent her a friend request. For one brief second, I thought, "What if she doesn't remember me?" But I immediately dismissed it. We were best friends! Of *course* she would remember me!

And she did. Shortly thereafter, I received a notification saying she had accepted my request. I was so excited! She is an art teacher *and* an artist *and* a business owner! She was celebrating an anniversary. There were pictures of her with small children (grandkids? nieces and nephews?), as well as links to her business. And as all this new information came in, I began to reflect on what her move had meant to me and how it had influenced the direction of my life.

I had been heartbroken when I learned she was moving. But with the benefit of hindsight, I see that some of the changes I made in my life shortly after her move would not likely have happened if she had stayed. It again reminded me that while not all things *are* good, all things can work *together* for good.

Stacey was not my only friend in sixth grade, of course, but she was my *best* friend, a top-tier friend. My other two primary friends, Amanda and Kelli, were more "second-tier" friends. That's not a judgment about their worth, of course; it simply means that they weren't my *best* friends. Top-tier friends are the ones with whom you can share anything without fear of judgment or betrayal. Their interests and values align with yours, and you just "click." Second-tier friends, on the other hand, are people you may share some interests with, but they're not the people with whom you bare your soul. Instead of having nine out of ten things in common with them, you might have six or seven. Logan calls them "light" friends, which I think is beautifully descriptive.

When Stacey moved, however, those two girls, by default, moved up to my first-tier friends. But they were never really as good a fit as Stacey; they weren't *true* top-tier friends. I never quite trusted my deepest thoughts and fears with them, and our interests never quite meshed in the same way.

Stacey and I were both involved in music. While Stacey played the flute and the piccolo, I played the clarinet (I wanted to play trumpet, but when you wear braces, that's not really an option). Amanda was in band, but it wasn't really her passion. Kelli was not involved in music at all.

Stacey and I were creative, although her creativity leaned more toward traditional visual arts like drawing and painting, while I leaned toward crafts, thanks in large part to my sixth-grade teacher, Sue Nystrom. After my dad died, Miss Nystrom let me hang out with her in her classroom at recess. She took her "break time" and invested it in teaching me the art of macramé and hairpin lace, and how to make cornhusk wreaths. I remember going with her to a crafts store to buy the materials for the wreath, and then having ice cream. Her extra attention meant the world to me, but I'm not sure teachers would be allowed to provide that extra kind of nurturing anymore.

But while Stacey and I were into art and crafts, Amanda and Kelli weren't. Stacey and I laughed and had fun together. Amanda was negative and always trying to "one-up" me, and Kelli once threatened to announce to Mr. Rittgers' science class that I had a (secret) crush on a particular boy—*in* the classroom, just before class started, with a loud, "Hey, everybody, guess what?" That kind of betrayal, which would have resulted in *utter* humiliation (it was seventh grade, after all), was not compatible with my idea of a good friend.

My father's death, Stacey's move and the attitudes and behaviors of my other "friends" created the perfect storm for change. It had been about 18 months since my father died. And research shows that, when children suffer a traumatic loss of a parent, whether through death, divorce or incarceration, they often make *huge* changes in their life at about that 18-month mark—which is exactly where I was when I changed friends.

I decided to completely switch my group of friends that summer between my seventh- and eighth-grade years. Which, as I look back at the timing, should have been daunting. Not only did I choose to switch groups in *junior high*, I chose to try to gain entry into the "popular" group. And I was decidedly *not* traditional, "popular girl" material. I had braces (and had, since the third grade). I wore ugly, octagon-shaped glasses (and had, since the fourth grade).

We didn't have a lot of money, so my clothes often came from Sears or JC Penney rather than the more trendy shops my prospective friends frequented. In short, my goal to be a part of that crowd should have appeared so impossible and farfetched as to stop me in my tracks and send me running back to my ill-fitting friends.

But for some reason, it never occurred to me that those girls might not accept me. I don't recall questioning my worthiness or wondering if I should have a back-up plan in case things didn't work out. My vision of what I wanted my high school years to look like was so crystal clear that I never once doubted it would happen. And contrary to most television sitcoms, I don't remember any of those girls rejecting me, taunting me or shunning me.

That could be because the popular girls in my class were *not* the "fast," partying, mean girls you see portrayed as popular in TV sitcoms. Instead, they were intelligent, involved in sports and music, and good kids. They were positive and ambitious. Wanting to be one of them meant that *I* had to change what I was doing, to be sure, but in a good way.

I became more active in school, trying out for spots on the eighth-grade cheerleading squad and the track team. I *hate* running, so the fact that I was willing to run track speaks volumes about how motivated I was to change my friends. Mr. Partington, the track coach, assigned me to the 800-meter race—I don't know *what* he was thinking. The only thing I lacked more than speed was endurance, so that "assignment" lasted for only one humiliating meet. I asked instead if I could run hurdles (why be like everyone else?), which was better but still involved *running*. But I stuck it out. In my house, you did not quit. It simply wasn't allowed. I didn't have to go out for track next year, but if I signed up *this* year, I was in it for the duration. And for that, I am grateful.

I was also a wrestling cheerleader in eighth grade. That year, our seventh- and eighth-grade wrestling squad went undefeated, and Mark Reese *pinned* every guy he wrestled! It was a heady time in the Johnston Middle School gymnasium, and we were loud and proud about it, playing Queen's *We Are the Champions* on my over-sized boom box after the final meet. Which would also probably not be allowed now, falling under the heading of "not being a gracious winner." I confess we weren't really concerned about the other team's feelings—we wanted to celebrate *winning*. That season was an incredible picture of hard work and accomplishment, and we believed that deserved a celebration.

In high school, I became even more active. I exchanged the dreaded track for tennis and added volleyball. I was a cheerleader, I was on the dance team and in every vocal music group the school had, whether as a singer or accompanist. I held a fun job and still made Honor Society. And I loved every crazy minute of it. Every new experience gave me confidence to join another organization or take part in a new extra-curricular activity.

At that time, Johnston was a unique school; it was small enough that you could participate in any and nearly every activity you wanted to, yet was close enough to the metro that you were never labeled a "hick" school. Working at Happy Joe's Pizza expanded my group of friends even further because it drew kids from all over the metro area. These were kids I never would have otherwise met, because kids from those big schools did not compete with our smaller school. I dated boys from Urbandale and Ankeny and Lincoln (the Lincoln guy was a definite mistake) and had friends from Hoover and Roosevelt.

When I initially wrote this chapter, I had framed all this change as the result of letting go of my previous friends. Stacey was an involuntary "let go," of course, but Amanda and Kelli were more affirmative "let go's."

But as I re-wrote the chapter, it occurred to me that my initial perception of letting go was a rather black-and-white concept. You either hung on tightly *or* you let go. Your metaphorical hands were either clenched in a fist of possession, or open, but flipped upside down, releasing everything. And neither of those positions—fist or flipped—allows new things to come *in*.

My situation with Amanda and Kelli didn't really fit neatly into either of those two options, which is why I struggled. It fell into that gray area between hanging on and letting go that I hadn't acknowledged existed. I didn't *force* Amanda and Kelli out of my life. Instead, I simply expanded my own opportunities for friendships with others.

Joining teams and choirs, staying involved in church and even my part-time job led me to new people, new experiences and new lessons. My interests and activities, as well as my ambitions for my life, differed from what Amanda and Kelli wanted or were willing to work for. These differences just naturally led to that shift in friends.

These kinds of natural shifts are, of course, true in adulthood as well. But for me, it has always been harder to let go of people as an adult. And in some respects, social media has made it even more of a challenge because it's so easy to stay connected, even when it might be better to let those relationships go.

I once told someone I liked Facebook because it allowed me to reconnect with my high school friends. With a sideways glance and a smirk, he said, "That's exactly why I'm *not* on it." He has a fair point. And yet, there are those whom I did not know well in high school who have become trusted long-distance friends. There are those whom I was friends with in high school, lost touch with in college and have now come back into my life (via Facebook), again as a close friend. There is something about friendship with those who have known you "forever and a day" that is different than new friends.

And now, after all these years, Stacey has returned to my circle. Her leaving, painful as it was, created the space and the circumstances I needed to grow into who I am today. I'm looking forward to reestablishing our friendship, although it will obviously look different than it did in sixth grade. She lives in Ohio, so we won't be hanging out at the coffee shop anytime soon, but I'm excited to hear about her life, and to catch up on what she's been doing.

Stacey's absence wasn't forever, although it did take a long time for her to wind back into my orbit. But some things are like that, and I'm grateful we've reconnected.

CHAPTER 23

HAIR (KIND OF)

Hair.
Yes, that's today's topic of discussion. I currently have long hair, but I am cutting it short—*pixie* short—next week. In fact, by the time this is published, it will be short (or long again, depending on when the book is published).

And that decision, of course, has me all worked up. My daughter's wedding is 13 months from now, and initially my plan was to keep it long for that event—so I could wear it up, of course. But it's driving me crazy, so I've decided to cut it. I can't go medium-length, because I have a weird wave in my hair that causes it to flip up when it's that length (when long, the weight pulls it straight; when short, it's not an issue).

I'm also tired of hearing that men like long hair because, well, you know (seriously—is *everything* about sex?). If that's what they're thinking when they look at me, it's hard to believe that they will take me seriously in a professional setting.

Despite this, I'm (mildly) freaking out. What if I have a serious case of "buyer's remorse"?

How ridiculous. It's *hair*, after all. It will grow back if I don't like it. And my hair grows fast. While "average" is ½ inch a month, mine grows ¾ inch a month—which over a year is significant. When I was pregnant with Logan, I had my hair cut three times, and each time I had *4 inches* cut off. It was still well below my shoulders when I had him, despite having had a full *foot* cut off during that nine-month time. So even at the non-pregnant growth rate of ¾ inch per month, it will grow nine inches by the time of Kierra's wedding. And I've had it short before and liked it.

I especially like the fact that it doesn't take me 30 to 45 minutes to do my hair in the morning when it's short (primarily because of how long it takes to dry that much thick hair when it's long).

As I'm wasting time and energy dithering over this, I receive an email from a dear friend who tells me that she was just diagnosed with breast cancer.

It stops me in my tracks. And somehow worrying about the length of my hair suddenly seems *sooo* trivial. I am ashamed of myself—and that's a good thing. Contrary to current thinking, not all shame is bad. And the irony that I am worrying about hair when she will lose hers is not lost on me.

Talk about perspective.

Michelle is one of the strongest women I know. She has already successfully battled cancer twice, as well as had a benign brain tumor removed a few years back. Unbelievably, she had the surgery at the University of Iowa Hospitals and Clinics on Friday, was out of intensive care on Saturday and went home to Waukee—a two-hour drive—on Monday. My husband, who was in the hospital for nine days for his heart surgery (seven of those in intensive care), jokingly complained that she was making him look bad.

Michelle is clearly no stranger to health issues and their challenges. Although there's no indication that her diagnosis is terminal, it nevertheless reminds me that at a certain point, we will all lose our battle to stay alive—some in our nineties, others as toddlers. Her diagnosis reminds me that I do *not* want to continue to live my life in fear mode, becoming paralyzed over even the smallest decisions.

I recently read a comment that when we start living into our gifts, we give God something to bless. When we don't take those steps, we stay stuck in fear, and there's nothing to bless. If I make a decision and it's the wrong one, I can always change. Think of it this way: if you get on a train to Chicago, and then decide Chicago is wrong, you don't have to *stay* in Chicago. You can catch another train and go somewhere else. And just because Chicago was a mistake, you don't have to stand at the ticket window unable to decide where to go, fearing that the *next* destination might also be a mistake. Just because Chicago was a mistake doesn't mean Denver will also be a mistake.

Life is a series of mistakes and course corrections. If we learn from these, we will eventually "hit" the right destination. But if we never even get on the train, we will *never* get where we are supposed to go. And we'll be miserable while we're stuck. Train stations, generally speaking, are not known for their aesthetics.

And why do we (ok, *I*) assume the *worst* outcome? Why don't I assume the *best* outcome? Instead of worrying that I might hate my hair, why not open myself up to the possibility that I might love it? And even if I do hate it, Michelle's diagnosis helps me realize that this decision, like most, is not a life or death decision.

⚔

Fast forward to 2015, a few years after I initially wrote about my hair. Michelle is post-chemo and radiation and is doing well. Her hair is back—and not her curly chemo hair, but her normal pre-cancer straight hair. Life is good.

Clearly, there are some "cats I need to bury." But I need to remember that not everything is so black and white, keep vs. let go, this direction vs. that, short vs. long. Is there a third, fourth or even fifth option? Is there a perspective I'm not considering, or some information I'm missing? Am I taking things too seriously or giving them too much weight and importance? What might happen if I held those things loosely, instead of in a vise-like grip or turning my hands upside down, ensuring they will "leave"?

Removing the life-or-death quality of these decisions also removes the associated stress and pressure to get it *just right*. It helps me make a decision in the first place, because the consequences aren't so dire—no matter what I choose. It permits me to make mistakes, viewing them as an opportunity to learn, rather than a disaster. I can be more relaxed, more confident and more proactive.

And I just might cut my hair again. But probably not *quite* so short this time.

CHAPTER 24

JUDGMENT

The comedian Gallagher once proposed a new traffic monitoring system that was not only hilarious, but also played right into my frustration with drivers who won't signal or go the speed limit, or the ones who cut you off or tailgate!

In Gallagher's world, everyone would be given a rubber-dart gun. When you saw someone being stupid, you would shoot his car with the dart, which would stick to the car *and* have a banner attached that reads "stupid." When there are multiple darts on a car, the cops would pull over the driver and write him a ticket for being stupid.

I could *totally* get behind that idea.

Unfortunately, I would want to use that same method on bad customer service reps, bad bosses/coworkers and politicians (ok, I know—low hanging fruit). I, of course, would *never* be shot with a dart, because clearly *I never* make a mistake (this is where a social media #sarcasm would be inserted, in case you didn't catch that with all the italics). And while I try very hard not to call people stupid, some of their actions just defy logic (or compassion)—unless you know the whole story.

My friend Bruce once said something very wise to me. He said, "We judge ourselves by our intentions and others by their actions." It's a good reminder that we all make mistakes and do stupid things—even (or sometimes especially) me. My intentions are usually good, even if my actions are not. I need to show others the same grace that is shown to me.

But it's also important to separate actions from the person; letting go of judgment doesn't mean I allow the behavior to continue.

I have (had?) a friend who works for the federal government. That means that we would often try to schedule time for coffee on federal holidays, which gave us a pretty wide selection of days. Now, normally she is a very responsible person. We set up a time to meet at West End Salvage (yes, that incredible place that was on HGTV) despite the fact that it was a bit of a hike for me, and the weather wasn't great that day (it *was* winter in Iowa, after all). But I showed up, despite the snow and ice (I am an Iow*an*, after all).

Unfortunately, she did not show up. Nor did she call.

I tried to reach her, but to no avail. Because I thought she was, by nature, a responsible person, I was worried that she had perhaps been in an accident. When she finally contacted me the next day, she told me that a friend's husband had died, and she was sitting with the wife. Which sounds like a completely reasonable reason for not meeting with me as planned—except that the man had died the previous *week*. Were there not 30 seconds in there *somewhere* where she could have texted me and said, "Sorry—something has come up and I can't meet on Tuesday"?

When we rescheduled, I chose a different location—one where I was planning to be anyway. That way, if she didn't show up, it wouldn't disrupt my plans. And you guessed it—she didn't show or call—again. I was amazed, and not in a good way. That evening, I got an email saying, "So sorry—I had *another appointment* and meant to email you. I'll call later." (Italics mine.) Another appointment?

She knowingly double-booked herself and then simply chose the other appointment over me? And then chose not to let me know? Well, now, *that's* a blow to the self-esteem.

And I am still waiting for her to email me as promised. And it's now July.

My first inclination was to judge her. What kind of a friend repeatedly pulls a no show/no call? What kind of a friend treats the relationship as though it's expendable?

I needed to stop judging her (because, of course, I have been guilty of standing people up, too, although in my case, it's usually because of a technology glitch—updates are not always my friend), but that didn't mean I had to continue to allow the behavior. I did not chase her down and try to reschedule. I did not ask what happened *this time*. I simply let it—and her—go.

Does this mean I will *never, ever talk to her again!* in the way of a first-grader who's been hurt by a friend who won't play on the merry-go-round at school? No. It just means that I am not going to make the effort to connect, and I'm not going to go out of my way to schedule her into my life. That's not judgment—that's just good old-fashioned boundary setting based on values and the type of friendships I want to cultivate. That's holding loosely, allowing friendships that are not serving me (or, apparently, her) to fall away naturally.

Maya Angelou once wrote that you should never make someone a priority who treats you like an option. Or, as one Pinterest pinner says, "Stop crossing oceans for people who wouldn't jump a puddle for you." Viewed through this lens, I began to see some interesting things.

I have friends in both camps: those who make our friendship a priority, and those who make it an option. That's fine—not every person I meet has to be a BFF who texts me every day just to see what's up. And it's not always about how often we get together.

It's more about the quality of the relationship and whether it's a *priority*.

I have some friends with whom I get together at least monthly, and who I talk to more often than that. Other friends may check in only sporadically, yet the quality of those conversations leaves no doubt in my mind that the relationship is a priority.

I've learned, too, that whether I am ending a friendship or simply letting it naturally downshift from a priority to an option does not mean I have to make a big deal about it. There's no reason I have to burn the bridge or tell people I'm "mad" at them for something they did that I don't happen to agree with or like. It's usually better to just let it go.

When I first began practicing law, I worked for a sole practitioner. We had an unconventional pay structure (and, from the 20/20 view of hindsight, financially ill-advised from my perspective). Ultimately I left because I realized that the pay structure was not much better than if I had my own business. For some reason that I can't remember now, I was upset with my boss. I could have easily burned that bridge, but I held my tongue. And I'm glad I did. He proved to be a good resource for me later, and I enjoy seeing him and catching up on what's going on with his family. I feel comfortable referring people to him, which benefits both him and the client and builds goodwill.

That doesn't mean I *never* speak up, of course. Because sometimes what I *think* is going on, or what I think someone's intentions are—aren't.

There was another woman who was a friend and former colleague who used to schedule time for coffee with me, and then, often at the last minute, reschedule because of a client conflict. Keep in mind this conflict arose *after* she had already scheduled time with me, *and* it was never presented as a "Would you mind..." ask but rather as an "I'm rescheduling our time..." tell.

Even the simple courtesy of asking instead of telling would have made a difference in how I felt about it. And because it would be highly unlikely for me to say, "No, you can't reschedule," the outcome would have been the same—a rescheduled meeting. What it felt like to me was that I was expendable. That work "always" came first for her (and I'm a bit sensitive to that paradigm), and that she thought I had nothing better to do than sit around and wait for her—as though everything *we* did revolved around *her* schedule (which happens a lot when you are self-employed, by the way).

I finally called her out on it. Her perspective on what was happening was completely different. She believed that because I was her "biggest cheerleader," I wouldn't mind if she canceled our coffee in order to build her business. It was a good example of how people who are "givers" (*see* Adam Grant's book *Give and Take*) sometimes get trampled on if they don't set boundaries.

I *was* very encouraging, but that didn't mean I wanted to be treated carelessly. Relationships are, I would argue, even more important than work. I believe this primarily because I believe that everyone is more successful at work if they invest in strong relationships. But the reverse is not necessarily true: investing in work doesn't necessary ensure successful relationships.

That doesn't mean that meeting someone for coffee or lunch always trumps work, of course. I totally get that from a time perspective; even those who are self-employed and have a more flexible schedule nevertheless have times where work has to take precedence. That does *not* mean work is, overall, a more important priority than relationship. But in this situation, it *did* feel like work was the higher priority, mainly because the "reschedules" happened multiple times. The relationship felt like a choice, where work was the primary consideration and I was an option.

I also totally get that I'm *not* going to be a priority for everyone I meet, and I'm completely okay with that. But what I am not willing to go along with is being told I am a priority, but shown I am an option. And common courtesy dictates (at least in my world) that canceling, with or without calling, should be the exception, not the rule.

Those are boundaries, not judgments. Once I removed the judgment and stuck to the boundaries, I was a lot happier. And boundaries allow the friendship to continue, whereas judgment does not.

CHAPTER 25

GOD

As I've written about earlier (several times, in fact—it was a big thing), I had a nasty run-in with God when my dad died. Or at least that's how I perceived it—as God hurting me, punishing me for something I couldn't understand. My brother and I had been fighting the day before he died. Nothing outside of normal sibling bickering, but when my dad intervened, his chest was heaving. Which meant nothing to me at the time, but I later wondered if our fighting had caused Daddy to have another heart attack. Were we responsible for his death? Was God punishing me for fighting with my brother? While I don't believe that now, it was a fearful thing to contemplate as a child.

When I was an adult, I read Maya Angelou's take on the saying, "God never gives us more than we can handle." Her response? A heartfelt, "I wish He didn't trust me quite so much." Amen, sister. Whether you agree with the initial sentiment or not, my dad's unexpected (to me) death was an awful lot for a 12-year-old to "handle." And I always wonder—what, exactly, does "handle" mean? Is anything short of suicide, deep depression, or mind-numbing substance abuse "handling" the situation? If it doesn't kill us, does it *really* make us stronger? Or does it eternally break us in some way?

My way of handling my mother's declaration that "God wanted your dad" was to first respond with the sarcasm that only a pre-teen can muster. I said (to myself), "Well excuse me, but I wasn't quite finished with him yet." I selfishly noted that God could have anybody's dad—why did he have to take *mine*?

Although well intentioned, my mother's words set me on a very destructive path in terms of my relationship with God. I was definitely angry with God. And then, of course, I felt immediately guilty. You weren't "allowed" to be mad at God, right? He was perfect, so anything He did had to be "right," yes?

I later "handled" it by allowing it to create a woe-is-me victim status that I unconsciously slipped into as a way to get people to feel sorry for me and be nice to me. I handled it by shutting down my feelings toward other people I loved, not wanting to experience that same level of excruciating pain if *they* "abandoned" me. I handled it by trying to make sure I could always take care of myself and my kids if something happened to my husband. I obtained two degrees—one in elementary education and one in law—so that I could always find a job. I didn't want to rely on anyone.

Not the best way to "handle" it, probably, but it was the best I knew how to do at the time.

It has been hard for me to trust God since my dad's death, mainly because I struggled to forgive Him. Just admitting that makes me think, "Are you *crazy*? Forgive *God*?" When people told me that God would take care of me no matter what, there was always a part of me that piped up, saying, "That's not true. He took your dad from you, remember? How is that taking care of you?"

When I asked for things in prayer, I often found myself saying, "I know You *can* do this; the question is *will* You?" As though I was challenging Him to fail me, so that I could say, "See? I was right. You don't really love me." I couldn't reconcile the concept of Him loving me with the "fact" that he had taken my dad from me at such an early age. So the natural conclusion was that He didn't love me.

In later years, it was even worse—I felt that God was indifferent to me. I would call out for help and hear—crickets. Nothing. Assuming God had not suddenly gone deaf, I could only blame His nonresponse on indifference. If he loved me, wouldn't he help me? And why *did* he "take" my dad from me?

Of course, it didn't occur to me that *I* might be the problem, reaching out only when I needed something, rather than spending time daily in prayer and meditation. And it didn't occur to me that my unresolved anger was the obstacle. I went to church like the good girl I was, but underneath, there was no foundation for those teachings to take hold. The thing that really kept me involved in church, that kept the thin lifeline between God and me intact, was music. That was the true value of the gift of music God had given me, although I didn't understand that at the time.

And then one day, when I was relating all of this (or, most all) to my mentor, he shook his head sadly and said just two words: "Bad teaching." He wasn't judging my mother; he knew she had done the best she could. I can't imagine how difficult it would be to tell your young children that the father they adored had died. *She* was also devastated and grief-stricken: a widow at 45 years of age.

I recently saw a T-shirt that read, "My daddy's so amazing that God made him an angel." I'm sure this sentiment was similar to what my mom was trying to convey—that God loved my dad so much that He just couldn't wait to get him to heaven. But that did not assuage my little heart-broken self. It just made me feel that God was selfish, punitive and uncaring. He had all the time in the world to take my dad to heaven—could He have not waited until I was an adult?

After my conversation with Curt, it occurred to me that I had been mad at God for a very long time for something that wasn't even true. My mother's teaching led me to believe that God had stolen my father from me, completely disregarding the fact that *I* still needed him—as though God had put his wants first, totally disregarding my needs. Who does that to a child? Well, while my CASA experience taught me that there are human parents who will hurt their children by putting their own needs and wants before those of their children, God does not.

I had to let go of that image of God and open myself up to the possibility of a different reason for my dad's death, a different story. Even though I knew I would never have used the "God wanted your dad" language with my own children, it didn't occur to me to apply that to my own experience. What would I have wished my mother to say to me? How could she have explained my dad's death in a way that comforted me and did not create this huge chasm in my relationship with God?

I was, and am, someone who needs to know—I need to know what happened and why. I have a hard time filing things in the mental folder labeled, "I don't know what happened or why" and leaving them there. "God took your dad" is not an acceptable reason to me. I needed to know more to appropriately process my grief, but I didn't know where to turn.

Logan has, for better or worse, inherited this particular trait from me. When 9/11 happened, he was barely nine years old. Way too young to watch the television images of planes crashing into buildings and people jumping to their deaths. But he knew *something* had happened—something unspeakably evil—and the not knowing what or why was stressing him out.

Although I was unwilling to let him watch the graphic television reports, I finally decided to let him read the newspaper while I sat near him, watching. He pored over every word, trying to make sense of what had happened. Witnessing his small body hunched over the paper, inhaling the words on the page and sorting them through his mind filled me with sorrow.

Like everyone else that day, I remember vividly where I was and what I was doing. The grief of that day is etched into memory, the disbelief and shock overwhelming. I did not want my nine-year-old to be exposed to such evil, but there it was, unavoidable and undeniable. I knew I couldn't protect him from everything, but it was a heartbreaking moment as a mother.

When he finished reading, there was a sense of calm. He at last knew what had happened—and what *hadn't*. He felt safer in the knowing, because even though it was a horrific and terrifying event, the not knowing was even scarier. He understood why the skies were silent, absent of planes.

He understood that while this had happened in the United States, it was not particularly close to where he lived. And he saw President Bush, Mayor Giuliani and thousands of others taking action, in both big and small ways to go after this evil and stop it. He was awestruck by the dedication of first responders and the lines at the blood donation centers and understood at the cellular level what it meant to be the *United* States of America.

When my dad died, there was nothing I could read that would help me know what had happened. JoAnn Zimmerman had not yet created her highly regarded Iowa nonprofit, Amanda the Panda, to help children process and understand death and the grieving process. Instead, it was left to my grieving and traumatized mother to explain something she herself didn't really understand.

Yes, she probably understood what *caused* his death, but understanding why this had happened to her? She probably didn't understand *that* part of it any better than I did. Years later, when Reverend Henry died, I spoke to his wife at the visitation. I told her what it had meant to us to have her husband's compassion and kindness during that dark time. She held my hand tenderly and said sadly, "Oh, that was one of the hardest things Charles ever had to do. There's just nothing that prepares you for having to tell a child her parent has died."

I think, too, that as parents, we feel like we have to know all the answers. Telling our children "I don't know" makes us feel like we have somehow let them down, especially when they are young. But it occurred to me that if my mother had said she simply didn't know why that had happened, that might have been better than assigning "blame" to God.

There are still things about which I have no answer. I've learned to simply say that. Sometimes it gets me in trouble because other people have such strong beliefs about things that lead me to say, "I don't know." But I always try to remember Mark Twain's sage wisdom in those situations: "It ain't what you don't know that gets you into trouble. It's what you know for sure that just ain't so."

I don't know whether my mom felt she "knew for sure" that God wanted to take my dad, or whether she was flying blind in the dark, hoping that those words would make me feel better, but I wish she had just said she didn't know why that had happened. I wish she had gone on to explain that we *don't* always know why things happen. Sometimes they will make sense down the road, and sometimes they won't, but we can drive ourselves crazy if we insist on trying to figure out everything.

When something happens to you as a child, you grow into adulthood carrying those childhood beliefs with you. There is no bright line where you suddenly say, "Ok—I'm an adult now. Which beliefs need to mature or change—overnight?"

Once I was able to let go of my image of God as selfish, uncaring and untrustworthy, I was able to open up to the possibility that, although not all things *are* good, all things can work *together* for good. I started seeing the strengths and perspectives that I would not have had without that experience.

Oddly enough, it's probably one of the reasons I am a feminist. At 12-years-old, I was mowing the lawn and assembling things like microwave carts that my mom bought but didn't know how to put together. I *had* to do those things: my dad wasn't around, and my brother was only nine. I knew at an early age that women and girls could do many, if not all, of the "boy" jobs; I knew it because I was doing it.

Letting go of my old image of God made it easier to let go of my dad as well, because I no longer felt like he had been "stolen" from me. Yes, it still felt unfair and tragic, but I was finally able to file the overall experience into that invisible, mental folder labeled "I don't know why that happened to me."

And that's finally okay.

And I'm amazed that God thought I was strong enough, even at 12, to trust me with that experience and my ability to handle it.

CHAPTER 26

BITTERNESS

We all have certain "skills" at which we excel but wish we didn't. For example, I tell people that although patience is *a* virtue, it's not really one of mine. My skill lies in *im*patience. And holding a grudge? There are few people who can match me in this area. Yesterday I saw a humorous list on Facebook that talked about how long people hold grudges based on their astrological sign. They ranged from .02 seconds for Libras (unless you really messed up) to "all of eternity" for Scorpios. Guess which one I am. Although I don't put my faith in astrological predictions (or Facebook lists, for that matter), this one was dead on.

I once worked for a relatively large company. Although I was only there for one year, I joked that it was about 364 days too many. People laugh when I tell them that, but there was more than a grain of truth to the statement.

This position was a newly created one. The company had astonished a number of consultants based upon how long they were in business before having a Human Resources department. They did, of course, have someone doing payroll and benefits, but there was no coordinated department handling things like recruiting, hiring/firing, or compliance. This company was driven heavily by operations, and rumor was that it feared that a human resources department would just get in their way.

Human Resources people are often seen as obstacles (the *real* party of no, according to people in operations) and a cost center, rather than a profit center. Operations people generally don't want HR people telling them what they can and can't do regarding hiring and, more important in this company, firing.

The man they chose to lead this newly created HR department epitomized this belief. He had been with the company for years and publicly stated his dislike for HR. From my perspective, he could not have been more ill suited for his position in HR. But from the company's perspective, it was likely thought that he was one of "them," and would "protect" them from *real* HR people and policies.

To be fair, Bill was one of those guys you either loved or hated—no gray area. So there were, I'm sure, people who liked him and his style of management. Yet Bill was not known for his compassion. I once was in a cell-phone store, and it turned out the guy behind the counter had once worked for him. When he found out I now worked for him, he shook his head and said, "That guy would slit your throat before he'd help you."

My perspective as a plaintiff's employment law attorney was, as you might imagine, a *bit* different about helping people. People who were encouraged and supported in the workplace are more loyal and more productive overall than those who are left to figure it out on their own. I saw what happened to companies when they made hiring/firing mistakes, and I understood why training was so important for both productivity and retention.

Even onboarding someone appropriately was critical, setting the tone for her whole employment experience. All of these things, if not done well, led to increased turnover, which was expensive. But at the point when I joined the "team," this company wasn't doing a lot of those traditional HR duties well, probably because they didn't really have an HR department.

My first sense of the amount of work to be done occurred on my very first day in the office. I arrived at my workstation to find I was assigned to a cubicle that had apparently been used for storage. The telephone was filthy. There was no computer and no basic office supplies. In short, there was nothing to indicate that they were either ready or excited for me to start.

I vowed that no one else would have that same experience. With the help of those connected to new hires, we created a process that ensured all new employees had a clean, welcoming workspace. Equipment was ready, supplies were in place, and there was a balloon bouquet to let them know we were happy they were there. New employees were given a tour (don't make them ask where the bathrooms are, please). We introduced them to people in the office, and they met with those who needed to help them do their paperwork. I lined up someone in their department to take them to lunch that first day and helped them set up their voice mail message.

The balloon bouquet turned out to have an additional, unforeseen purpose. I noticed that people were not taking them home for several days. I thought perhaps they didn't like them, but when I finally asked someone about it, they said, "I leave them here because it's the only way I can find my desk!" It hadn't occurred to me that in a sea of cubicles, those brightly colored helium balloons provided a low-tech "GPS," reducing the stress of getting lost in unfamiliar surroundings.

This whole process helped the people connected to new hires as well. Before, the IT people might receive an email saying someone was starting "tomorrow" and would be asked to have a computer ready for them. This could sometimes be challenging because there weren't always extra computers just waiting to be used. And the setup was different depending on what that individual needed.

The hiring process now included a requirement that the person doing the hiring send me a form about the new person. From there, I sent the information to everyone who had anything to do with onboarding, whether it was the IT department, the people who created the keys, the custodial staff, the people who did the paperwork or anyone else. They now had plenty of time to get everything ready.

My boss and I also had very different styles. I was the big picture, strategic planning, process-makes-things-easier one, and he was the operational, jump-in-and-just-do-it person. I wanted to avoid obstacles at the outset; he preferred to cross those bridges when (not if) we came to them. I wanted to figure it out *once* at the beginning, rather than deal with the same problem every time it came up. I wanted to make sure that what we were doing lined up with the company's stated vision and strategic plan; he wanted to simply make decisions based primarily, if not solely, on numbers. Besides the fact that this did not allow for different growth rates or personalities, it also caused difficulties when he would try to make "tools" do things they weren't designed to do.

I remember when an outside consultant was trying to sell him on the DiSC assessment. It's a personal assessment tool that's designed to help people discuss and understand behavioral differences. But that's not how Bill wanted to use it. He wanted to have the top supervisors take the assessment, and then use those results as a hiring tool. He wanted to hire people whose profiles matched those of the current high achievers.

No matter how many times the consultant and I tried to explain that this was not a valid use of the assessment, he insisted it would work. When the results came back showing that the successful supervisors all had *completely different profiles,* it was all I could do to refrain from saying, "We told you so."

There are many different ways to be successful—there rarely is a single "best practices" personality (although some professions may tend to draw people with certain personalities or strengths). Bill wanted a quick and easy way to know who to hire, rather than a more nuanced approach to supporting the people who were there, which required more effort. Bill decided the assessment was a failure (which was true in the sense that it didn't do what he wanted it to do; i.e., predict good hires) and decided against using it.

There are other assessments that I find to be more helpful in the workplace, but no assessment will "work" if you try to use it for something that it's not designed to do.

I told people that if I had managed Bill, rather than the other way around, we might have been successful. Not because I knew more than he did or was smarter than him, but because of the different nature of our strengths. My strengths aligned more with strategy and vision, and his with implementation. I could have told him what the vision and the goals were, and he would have been happy as a clam making that happen. As it was, putting the two of us together with him supervising me was like the proverbial water and oil—and then throwing a match on top.

After a year so stressful that I suffered migraines and multiple bouts of bronchitis (lowered immune system due to stress would be my guess), I finally "let go" of that job. I had no other job lined up, and some thought I should stick it out until I found something else, but I knew that my physical and mental health would not be able to take much more.

I had been so excited to start! Because it was a new position, I thought there would be the potential to create and do some great things. It was easier to let go of the position when I realized that was never going to happen. Although it was easy enough to let go of the *position*, I had (and still struggle with) a difficult time letting go of the bitterness and resentment. I joked that it was a good thing I had "7x70" times to forgive my boss, because it was probably going to take every single one of those "opportunities" for forgiveness.

But I confess I was not trying really hard, either. I didn't want to forgive him because that felt like I was sending the message that it was okay to treat people the way he had treated me. It was righteous anger, which is the hardest kind to let go of because as the name implies, you are so *right*. You want everyone to know that whatever happened was *not your fault*, and you want other people to take your side and be just as angry with the other person as you are.

But it can complicate things.

A few years after I quit, Jack, one of the few executive level people I actually liked at the company, died. For some reason, his funeral was very difficult for me. Even when Jack and I disagreed, we remained friends. It was never personal, and I don't remember ever exchanging harsh words with him. He was a wonderful person who died way too young.

His funeral was at a large church, and there was a section reserved for company employees. Even though I no longer worked there, my husband did, so he and I sat in the reserved section. And guess who sat behind us? You guessed it—my former boss. At one point in the service, everyone was asked to greet those around us with a handshake and "Peace of Christ." As an introvert, I'm always uncomfortable with those things. Add to that the sorrow I felt over Jack's death and my still-simmering anger about how I had been treated, and you can probably see where this is going. I confess—I deliberately snubbed my former boss. I just could not bring myself to extend that grace to him at that moment. But immediately, I thought, "I'm going to hell. I just snubbed someone in church." Not my finest moment.

A week or so later, I decided I had to apologize. I didn't like Bill anymore than I had before the funeral, but what I had done at the funeral was clearly wrong. Sitting across from my husband in the coffee shop, I wrote an email, telling Bill that although working for him had been one of the worst experiences of my life (okay, I didn't phrase it *exactly* like that), what I had done at Jack's funeral was wrong, and I apologized. When I read the email to Randy, his eyes grew wide, and he said, "Are you going to actually *send* that?!"

"Yes," I said, as I hit send. Whatever faults Bill had, I will say that I could always shoot straight with him. And it was really no big secret that I had not been happy working for him.

I heard nothing for several days. *Typical,* I thought, rolling my eyes in disgust.

Then a few days later, I took Randy to work. Bill apparently saw me, although I honestly did not see him. He finally responded to my email, stating that my poor experience had largely been his fault, and that I was a good person. I nearly fell off my chair. I had to reread it several times to make sure I hadn't misread something. He went on to say that he hoped I would somehow find it in my heart to forgive him.

My experience with him had been so bad that my first thought was, *Who are you, and what have you done with Bill?* Even now, I wonder if his secretary wrote it and sent it to me, unbeknownst to him.

That email did not cause me to suddenly change how I felt about him, and there are still some days when I can't even say that I have completely let go of the bitterness I felt. The hurt was too deep, perhaps, to ever let it go completely. However, I have a new resolve to no longer dredge up those negative feelings or allow the experience to "live rent free" inside my head. I don't want to continue holding that anger because I have more important, more *positive* places to focus that energy.

So maybe I haven't been holding the grudge for all eternity, but after *10 years,* it feels like it. Let. It. Go.

CHAPTER 27

LIGHT FRIENDS

Kylie is back!
Kylie is not a family member, a BFF, or someone I went to school with. I don't work with her, go to church with her, or work out with her. No, Kylie is a barista. One of my favorite baristas, to be precise. My favorite coffee shop is a place called *Grounds for Celebration*. It's owned by Jan and George, who have three retail locations, as well as a coffee farm in Panama.

George can wax poetic about coffee, while Jan is the tea expert. Megan runs a tight ship in their absence, telling people their dogs can't come in (unless they're service dogs), caring little if they're mad. She's not rude about it, but it is the law, after all.

George and Jan roast their own coffee at one location and bake their own pastries at another. The people who frequent their establishments are often regulars and become acquaintances and sometimes friends. Some people regularly move tables and chairs around to suit their needs (usually the local Democrats on Monday, the Bible study group on Wednesday morning, and the retired teachers Wednesday at lunch), while others snag the comfortable chairs in front of the fireplace for a cozy place to read.

When Kylie left for a year-long adventure teaching English in Spain, they bought a journal and had everyone who either worked there or was a regular customer sign it with their best wishes for her. But in addition to signing our names, we were to write down our "regular" drink. Although most days I order a dark roast coffee, I signed my "name" as *Friday caramel latté,* because that's what she would recognize. It's my special treat for that day. This is so well known that one barista jokingly refused to sell me a caramel latté one day because it wasn't a Friday! Hilarious.

Some of these baristas become what my son calls "light friends." Kylie is one of those. Liz (the latté police referenced above) is another. Brittany and Amber are my Sunday go-to girls, and Lily rounds out my list of favorites. They joke with me, ask about my kids and commiserate over the vagaries of life.

And they leave.

They leave because they're at that age where life is inviting them to go on great adventures. Kylie was teaching in Spain for a year. She's home for the summer, and then back she goes to a different area of Spain in the fall. Liz joined the Air Force, and Brittany will be heading to Utah in the fall. When they leave to go to far-off places for adventure, I head down to Raygun for their gifts.

Raygun was started by Mike Draper when, as he puts it, "his last hope of having a respectable life was extinguished." But don't let that fool you. Raygun is a thriving small business, with locations in Des Moines, Iowa City and Kansas City. It recently got a great shout-out from *The New York Times*. What does this "great last hope" of a retail store sell?

Snarky, hilarious T-shirts. And other memorabilia, such as magnets, postcards, and koozies. They're irreverent and range from the political statements (caucus T-shirts commemorating Iowa's first-in-the-nation status are hot now) to sports commentary (ISU's basketball coach just left to become the coach for the Chicago Bulls, and one of their "overheard in the store" comments was "Damn, we forgot to clip his wings like the swans at Lake LaVerne"), to social issues (whenever another state passes gay marriage, a new T-shirt comes out proclaiming that that state is now "as gay as Iowa."). Much of it is local snark, the kind that pokes fun in a funny rather than mean-spirited way.

So when my little barista "sistahs" leave, I head down to Raygun and stuff a small gift bag with things to help them remember home. I buy the postcard that says "IOWA—75% vowels, 100% awesome." The magnet that says "Iowans: The few, the proud, the extremely attractive." And finally, the koozie that proclaims "Des Moines: Hell Yes." They're fun, they're kitschy and perhaps even a good conversation starter for the former baristas in their new "home."

These girls all stay connected, and then those who are still here update me on those who are not. Yet with the exception of Brittany, I don't know any of their last names (I only know Brittany's because I connected her to my daughter, and it was in her email address). That's true of some of the regulars as well. I know Ron and Scott and Francis, and Tammy (who borrows my pen and doesn't want to return it) but others I recognize by face only.

But the coffee shop isn't the only place I have "light" friends. On Thursdays, I go to the Manhattan Deli. It's a small deli in an older building that looks like they didn't take down the wall when they expanded; they simply cut a door at one end, and a bigger door at the other.

The tables have the necessities (napkins, salt and pepper), and nothing more. The space behind the counter is crowded with the guys rushing to make sandwiches for the people lined up at the door, while the woman at the register rings up the orders and makes small talk while people fish out their money (cash or check only—no debit or credit cards accepted here, in case you were thinking of heading down for a sandwich).

Because I only go on Thursdays (for that day's special), and because I always get the exact same thing, the guys start making my lunch before I've even placed my order. Sometimes it's ready before I've finished paying! They see me walk through the door and just start making the order.

Steve, Fred, and James work there (and Garrett used to), but I don't know their last names. They know my first name because it's on my ticket. I had to eavesdrop or actually ask to learn their names. But I'm just as likely to be called "sweetie" as my name—and I'm okay with that. There's a relationship there, even though it's a light one, which makes it perfectly fine.

Not everyone can be a BFF, nor should they. These light relationships add to our life without overwhelming us with commitments of either time or effort. I don't expect Liz to email me from wherever she is stationed. I don't expect Garrett to call me about his new job. I was happy to see Kylie yesterday and briefly hear about her time in Spain, but I didn't scold her for not sending me a postcard. That's not the relationship.

My church friends are a little bit like that. I've gotten to know a number of people at Plymouth Church (Plymouth Congregational United Church of Christ, if you want to be technically correct, though members rarely exert that much effort), mainly through serving as a Deacon for three years and a choir accompanist longer than that. The adults I've met through choir start off as "Sage's mom," or "Shea's dad." If I'm lucky, I figure out their actual names before the year is over—just in time to be faced with a new group of kiddos and their parents!

As a Deacon, I am more likely to recognize faces than know names (unless people have their nametags on). Both "deaconing" and serving as the choir accompanist puts me at a bit of a disadvantage; people often know my name, but I may not know theirs. I'm always grateful when someone recognizes my deer-in-the-headlights look and tells me her name.

But although I may (or may not) know my church people better than my baristas, it's still rare that I would spend time with them outside of church. It's not that I don't like them, of course. Part of it is simply the fact that I am an introvert. Socializing can sometimes be exhausting for me.

Tonight I'm going to a potluck for the Deacons. The June potluck is always a bigger mix of people: the ten deacons (and their spouses) who are coming off the board, the twenty deacons (and their spouses) who are still on the board (it's a three-year term), and the ten deacons who are just coming onto the board (and their spouses).

Although not everyone can make it, it's still a *lot* of people for someone like me. And I'm already dreading it. It reminds me of the meme: "Go to the potluck, they said. It will be *fun*, they said." And I'm sure it will be fine, but I am equally sure I will be ready for bed when I get home (update—it really *was* fine; beyond fine, in fact, but at 8:30 my introverted self said, "Time to go home.").

The other part is that I'm someone who tends to compartmentalize her life. I have church friends, family friends, barista friends and work-related friends, and I seem to take the attitude that ne'er the twain shall meet. I don't know *why* I'm this way—I just am. What that means is, I see my barista friends at the coffee shop, my Manhattan Deli friends at the deli, my church friends at church... you get the drift.

Beyond that, though, these are all examples of friendships I've *naturally* held loosely. The people drift in and out of my life, and certainly I miss them when they leave, but I don't fret about it. While in my life, they add meaning and flavor; they smooth out the rough edges and make me feel like I matter in some small way. They make me feel like I might be missed if I didn't show up one day.

When Liz was still here, there were a few days when I wasn't at the coffee shop. When I finally showed up, she said (quite loudly),

"Jean! Where have you *been*?" She was clearly "offended" that I had not been there for a while. And I have to say, it made me feel good. We all want to think that someone would miss us if we didn't show up. But interestingly, it doesn't always have to be the people with whom we have the deepest relationships.

Sometimes it's just as heartwarming when it's the barista.

CHAPTER 28
WHO DEFINES ME?

I can count on one hand the television shows I routinely watch, but one of them is *Rehab Addict,* hosted by Nicole Curtis. Although I love watching the transformation of old "death row" homes, a perhaps bigger part of why I watch it is because of Curtis herself. I love watching strong women in non-traditional roles like construction/renovation. She has a fun, quirky sense of humor. She's passionate about saving old homes. But most of all, I like her outlook on life. No matter what disaster (burst pipes, fried power lines and pay-at-the-pump card *readers* that turn into card *eaters,* to name a few), she grouses about it for a minute and then says, "The good news is..."

This consistent optimism is what keeps moving her forward when lesser men would quit. But it's unlikely that she would have developed that attitude without a strong belief in who *she* is and what she's about. *She* defines herself—she does not let others define her. And those are both lessons I need to take to heart.

I sometimes need to let go of my assumptions about whether something is good or bad. I need to remember my mentor's admonition that "nothing is all good, nothing is all bad," and look for the good—the opportunities—rather than assuming the worst. I believe you often find what you are looking for, so why wouldn't I want to look for good? And why would I let other people define me? Do I think they know me better than I do?

I once met with the head of Human Resources at Meredith Corporation. Meredith, as most all Des Moines people know, is a big publishing company. Their flagship publication is *Better Homes and Gardens*, although they have many other magazines as well. One year, when I was at the point where I did not want to practice law, I decided I wanted to write. A magazine publisher seemed like a good place to look for a writing job (yes, it's a "Captain Obvious" kind of statement).

When I met with the HR Director, I explained all this to her. We spent an hour talking, during which time I *repeatedly* told her I did *not* want to practice law. I explained why. I told her why I wanted to change and why writing would be a good fit. But at the end of the hour, she said, "Well this has been delightful! But probably the best place for you is the legal department."

What?!

Why would the *best* place for me be the place I repeatedly said I didn't want to be? It defies logic. I understand her perspective— my law degree said I should go to the legal department. My lack of either a journalism or English degree said I could not be a writer. Both completely logical. And completely *wrong*. But she was the *director of Human Resources* with a *publishing company*, so surely she was the expert. And that willingness to assume she knew better than me caused me to set aside my dream of being a writer again. It set me back in pursuing my dreams. That wasn't her fault, though; I allowed it.

I also let people define who I am and what I can do by making incorrect assumptions about how much experience I have to have before someone will hire me.

At one point, I was doing some work for a start-up organization. I happened to be in their office one day when a young man (who appeared to be right out of college, but I could be wrong—the older I get, the younger young people look) was getting ready to do a presentation for them. I was invited to sit in on the presentation and provide input.

It was an eye-opening experience. This man was quite—confident. He showed them what he had written in response to their request for a sample writing that would tell their "story," and I was appalled. From a legal standpoint, there were certain things he should not have included. But beyond that, the tone was negative and didn't necessarily send the message I thought they wanted to send (having worked with them for a while). Yet here he was, saying, "I can do this." All I could think was, "No, you can't, at least not yet. But *I* can. And I can do it *now*." And then I found myself wondering why *I* hadn't suggested I do that for them.

Instead of telling them how I could best help them, I had waited for them to tell me what they wanted me to do. And I had assumed that they wouldn't hire me to write for them, because I didn't have a lot of *paid* experience with my writing. Seeing that young man confidently sell himself and ask for business while I sat on the sidelines waiting to be asked was a lesson I needed to see. The fact that I was reading Sheryl Sandberg's book *Lean In* just made it all the more glaring.

I let people tell me I couldn't be a coach without a coaching certificate. But when I just went out and *coached*, I had a great experience. I loved it, and my very first client told me how good I was! Did she care about the certification? No. What she cared about were results.

Curt once told me that one of the biggest obstacles I faced was my unwillingness to break the rules. Following the rules leads to great success in school, but not too far beyond that. I'm not talking about breaking the *law*, of course. I'm talking about breaking the "ought to" rules, the ones that keep us in our "place," the ones that make other people comfortable, but bore us to tears and frustrate us in our pursuit of a great life.

And I unfortunately let people I care about influence my decisions about personal issues, usually in the context of faith. I fail to make the decisions I should because I don't want to disappoint "them." I see that they have a strong faith and appear to know what they're talking about when it comes to what God wants. Yet their solution doesn't seem right for my situation. But I still go along, assuming they have the "right" answer, all the while allowing myself to be perfectly miserable in order to not risk losing a friendship or God's favor.

At a certain point, I quit asking for what *I* wanted. As I look back, this happened when others (people of influence) suggested that to ask for what you want, especially if that something is a material thing or success as "society" defines it, is selfish or greedy. And this idea of asking for what you *need,* not what you *want* is driving me crazy. Maybe I don't need something in a purely survival-mode sense, but does it not count if I "need" something to live my life a particular way?

Yesterday's sermon was about life in transition (it was graduation Sunday, after all), but I suspect that the part that most caught my attention was not the minister's primary point (which I can't even remember now). The part that was most memorable was the comment about the challenges of this "in-between time" that bridges high school and college. Yet graduation is not the only "in-between" time we find ourselves in throughout life. In fact, the sermon felt particularly relevant to where I am now.

The sermon included a story from the television series *Friday Night Lights.* I've never seen the show (not one of the handful I watch) and really know nothing about it, but the story that was part of the sermon was about a woman named Tyra. Tyra has grown up in an environment where it would seem her options would be limited. Her closest role models are not *good* role models. Money is an issue. But people stepped into her life and encouraged a different outcome for her.

In writing her college essay, she wrote, "Two years ago, I was afraid of wanting anything...But now I find I can't stop wanting." She proceeds to list a number of these wants. Some of her wants are about things she wants to do; others are things she wants to have and, most important, who she wants to be.

In a statement far wiser than her years would suggest, she states, "I want to define myself instead of having others define me." She concludes by saying that it's not that she thinks she's going to get all these things simply because she wants them. But it's the *possibility* of getting them that drives her desire to go to college.

Although I'm obviously not a graduate looking toward college, I am, nevertheless, in one of those in-between times. A time where I need to be making some hard decisions that have uncertain outcomes, as the minister observed. A time where I need to let go of being defined by others and instead hold tightly to my ability to define myself. A time to go after my wants, and let go of the belief that this is somehow selfish. A time to let go of framing things in the negative, and instead, look for the opportunity.

The good news is, there are endless opportunities.

CHAPTER 29

LAW

After my miscarriage years ago, it wasn't long before I was pregnant again. I had applied for a temporary job, and I did not reveal that I was pregnant (it was a *temporary* job, one that would be over before I would need maternity leave, so who would care?), and I wasn't showing. But then the office manager who interviewed me explained that although the position was temporary, the hope was that if the person hired "worked out," a permanent position would be offered. Now I was in a bit of a quandary. Should I tell? Ultimately I decided not to. It would have been illegal for them to ask, so I was under no obligation to tell.

I was hired and began working as a receptionist and secretary. The woman who had interviewed me was both the office manager and the administrative assistant for the attorney/owner. But there were two sole practitioners who also shared space with this attorney. I provided administrative support for them as part of their agreement with the owner. They were not, however, *employees* of the owner.

I was glad I did not support the owner. He was arrogant and rude—all the things people hate about lawyers. When he was playing golf, he wanted me to tell callers that he was "in depositions."

That was a lie, so I refused to say that. I simply said he was out. But his little deception about where he was and what he was doing was apparently well known in the legal community. One day, when he actually *was* in depositions, another attorney called. I told him Mr. Smith was in depositions. The attorney laughed and said, "Oh— out playing golf today, huh?"

I didn't have a lot of contact with Mr. Smith, and I liked the attorneys I did support. Things were going well, and I was expecting to be offered the permanent position any day. My pregnancy had, however, begun to show by then.

One day, another woman came in and said she had an interview with Kathy. I learned she was interviewing for *my* position. After she left, I went into Kathy's office. She tried to ignore me. When it became apparent I was not going to leave, she looked up from her game of computer solitaire and asked what I wanted. I said, "You promised me that job if I worked out. I've done a great job here; why are you considering other people?" Without batting an eye, she said, "You should have told us you were pregnant," and returned to her game.

Apparently, she didn't get the memo that pregnancy discrimination is illegal.

The firm was too small to sue (very small companies are not typically covered by anti-discrimination statutes like Title VII), so that option was not open to me. I will say, though, that the karma was strong with this one. A few years later I learned that the office manager went to prison for embezzling funds from the firm. But while that gave me some emotional satisfaction, it did not restore my job.

I was not to be completely thwarted, though. I took a different, rather unorthodox path—I decided to go to law school. I would practice employment discrimination law and teach those big, bad companies a *lesson* about how to treat their employees! I would be SuperLawyer, out to avenge all those who were discriminated against. If I couldn't help myself, I would help others. I had the grandiose and mistaken belief that I would *always* win, because I had *justice* and *fairness* on my side!

While that could have been the pregnancy hormones talking, my passion (and indignation) was so great, it blinded me to the practical realities—and the red flags that were popping up everywhere. First, my information materials got lost in the mail (this was before the internet and email). By the time I received the materials, I was bumping up against deadlines.

I needed to take the LSAT, but I didn't have the money for that. Undaunted, I found a school that would waive the fee for me. We were living in Omaha at the time, but I wanted to go to school at Drake in Des Moines (no *way* was I staying in Omaha to go to Creighton). I assumed we would be living there soon, so I signed up to take the LSAT in Des Moines.

We weren't.

I took our two *young* children (my son was only a few months old) and drove alone to Des Moines, staying with my brother- and sister-in-law. Logan was up several times in the night, and so I went into one of the most important exams of my life utterly exhausted. My score turned out to be good enough to get in, although I joke that what really got me in was diversity. I was an "old" student at 29, and female. Well—that and the incredible recommendation letter my former boss at the University of Iowa wrote.

But even my acceptance was a challenge. In yet another USPS snafu, my acceptance letter got lost in its own version of March madness, going all the way to FLORIDA ("for spring break, perhaps?" she asks with a bit of snark). I began getting voice mails welcoming me to Drake Law School. Since I hadn't gotten the letter, I thought it was some kind of sick joke. The letter finally arrived, mangled and postmarked to within an inch of its life.

To me, all of this proved the power of perseverance. Despite obstacle after obstacle, I had overcome. I was going to law school. Life was good.

But life wasn't done trying to tell me that this wasn't one of my best moves. When I started law school, my husband did not yet have a job in Des Moines, so the kids and I moved ahead of him. Did I mention that the year I started law school was also the year of the great flood of 1993? We literally could not find a place to live because the streets were so flooded you could hardly get anywhere. We moved in with my mother-in-law Martha (who owned a *two-bedroom condo*) because she had water. Although I'm grateful that she took us in, this arrangement did not go especially well.

I remember one particular incident. Although Kierra had inherited a lot of my "goody-two-shoes" genes, she was still a three-year-old. One evening, she was "expressing" her displeasure with one of my decisions—*loudly*. Martha jumped off the couch, eyes blazing, going after *my* daughter. I stopped her mid-stride, my own mama grizzly eyes shooting fire, and said, "*I* will handle this." She saw something that made her stop and sit down. I knew she was concerned about disturbing her neighbors, but I was not going to let her "discipline" my child.

Martha was, over all, a wonderful, generous mother-in-law. In her later years, when she was ill, she would tell anyone who would listen how thankful she was to have two such wonderful daughters-in-law. But those weeks we spent living there, with all the challenges of the move, the flood, getting used to daycare and law school—well, it was difficult for *all* of us, and it's another experience I wouldn't want to repeat.

When water was restored to my mother's neighborhood, we moved in with her because she had a three-bedroom house, a yard and no upstairs neighbors to disturb. But it was still months before we were able to find our own place and get my husband back together with us. When people ask me how I did all that, I simply reply, "If I wanted to go to law school, I didn't have a choice. I just did what had to be done, putting one foot in front of the other."

Then came year two, and I began having panic attacks. The first one came during a civil procedure class where we were talking about rape shield laws. My heart started racing, and I felt like I was going to faint. Despite the fact that I had been participating in the conversation, I pulled my things together, got up and *left*. I just had this overwhelming need to get out of that room.

When I later went to my professor's office to apologize for leaving so abruptly, she told me that she's always a bit hesitant to talk about the topic, because she does not know what experiences people have had. In today's lingo, she would be talking about "triggers." I told her that this was not the case with me, and that I didn't know *why* this had happened.

It happened again in an ethics class, and there were several other times when I had milder attacks. Yet I was in too deep to simply quit. I had ignored the signs about not going to law school, and I was paying a heavy price.

Year three brought the challenge of the bar exam. Prior to that, I had to attend a two-week bar review course in Iowa City, which meant I was away from my kids for longer than I ever had been. I remember taking a break from studying one evening to watch *Law & Order*. This was the original series and must have been Season Six.

Jill Hennessey played Assistant D.A. Claire Kincaid. The episode that night was a particularly dark one, dealing with the death penalty. All who had a part in the man's conviction were trying to deal with the ramification of their role and his sentence. Although believing that they did the right thing in arresting and convicting him, they are clearly not as comfortable with being held "responsible" for the *sentence*.

Claire alone is able to articulate this in a way that could have led to a healthy dialogue. But in a horrific plot twist, Claire is killed by a drunk driver while driving Detective Briscoe home. Given my emotional state, the separation from my kids, and the high anxiety level regarding the upcoming exam, I actually felt traumatized by this ending and never watched the show again.

Finally, the first day of exams arrived. My class was the last one to take the all-essay version of the exam—after that, they went to the Multi-State Exam. The exams were all-day Monday, all-day Tuesday, and a half-day on Wednesday. Typically you had your results by the end of that week, which is unheard of now. Each half-day session contained seven questions. You chose five to answer, and with the exception of the ethics question (which you were required to answer), you got to decide which five.

There were many strategies flying around about how to best approach that, but regardless of strategy, it was an incredible amount of material to learn, remember and apply in such a short time. You had to be fingerprinted, and you had to have your I.D. with you at all times. If you went to the bathroom and then tried to come back in, you had to show your I.D. The stress was palpable, and I remember sitting in the front row and hearing someone actually *crying* behind me. Talk about discouraging!

When the results were posted, they were equally stress-inducing. They posted your number, of course, rather than your name, but for some reason, they chose to post your number if you *failed* rather than passed. I do not know whose evil idea that was, but it does align with the research that says law is the only profession in which a negative attitude is a plus.

Also, the numbers were not posted online, they were on a sheet taped to the window of the law school. You dreaded walking up to look, but you also *needed* to look as quickly as possible. You hoped that if you failed, you could put on a winning poker face so no one would know.

It was even worse for those who failed this particular June exam, because the switch to a multi-state exam in December meant that if you failed in June, you didn't even have the benefit of experience to help you with the December exam. My heart went out to those who failed (24% of those who took the exam), but I was simultaneously grateful that I wasn't one of that 24%. I passed the Iowa Bar Exam.

Despite all the trials and tribulations, I had survived. Battle scarred and newly cynical, I had "triumphed." But the worst was yet to come.

I hated the practice of law.

But I couldn't just *quit*. I had too much time and money invested in it to just quit, right? So I tried different things. I tried having my own firm. I tried working part-time. But while those things helped, none addressed the basic problem—I hated the actual work. Having my own firm or practicing part-time was just doing what I hated in different ways, or in fewer hours. It didn't change the work itself.

Then my husband was offered a job in Colorado. Suddenly, I had my escape! I wasn't licensed in Colorado, so I *couldn't* practice law. I could quit without it being my *fault* (there it is again)! I felt such a sense of relief. Until a few months later when I realized that I also hated living in the mountains. For those of you who are asking, "How could *anyone* hate living in the mountains?" I will simply say this: I couldn't breathe (we were at around 9,000 feet). It took 45 minutes to just get down the mountain, let alone where you were going after that. I couldn't cook (water boils at a much lower temperature at 9,000 feet, so it takes forever for anything to cook). And we had bears on our deck. *Bears.*

My mom's cancer came back, and here I was, ten hours away. Fortunately, I was homeschooling the kids (which I loved!), so traveling back when necessary wasn't a problem. The kids and I would just pack up the car and go (although they weren't old enough yet to help drive, so it was all me). But we couldn't keep doing that.

A new opportunity appeared for Randy in Des Moines, and we leapt at it. Well—I did, anyway. I was again looking for external situations to solve problems I had gotten myself into trying to escape *other* problems. It wasn't that the opportunity would have been bad; it's just that it wasn't as developed as we were lead to believe. The kids and I moved back to Des Moines on Thanksgiving (that move is a story in and of itself), but once again, Randy's employment hadn't caught up.

But what about *my* work? Even though I didn't want to practice law, I still liked telling people I was a lawyer. It was an achievement of great pride for me. During the course of the next few years, I occasionally tried to get back "in"—usually when I was desperate for income. But every time I tried, weird things happened. I finally gave up.

In 2015, I started doing some consulting work around the idea of retention/ recapturing high talent—specifically, talented women. Forgetting that I had "given up on law," the consulting work led me to the idea that law schools and the continuing legal education (CLE) events needed to be different, more practical. I approached my alma mater about this, and the associate dean was very encouraging—right up until the day before we were to present to the dean. Suddenly, the whole thing was off.

I tried a different approach, meeting with a woman who was well connected to various legal organizations. Guess what happened here. I missed *two* meetings with her! I *never* do that—but I would put the meeting on my calendar, and then the day of the meeting it wasn't there anymore.

I gave up—again. I let go of trying to work in the area of law, whether as a lawyer or consultant. It seemed like every time I got close to the profession, the most bizarre things happened. Talk about burning bushes!

What happened next was what often happens when I finally let go. Things come right back, but in a way I wasn't able to see when I was clutching them so tightly in my hands.

I was at church one Sunday, serving as a Deacon, when my friend Hallie, a fellow deacon *and* attorney, said, "I signed up for the PCWA (Polk County Women Attorneys) luncheon on Wednesday because I saw you were speaking." I looked at her questioningly. "Really?" I asked. It was pretty clear I had no idea what she was talking about. We confirmed with another female attorney (yes, there are a lot of us at Plymouth) that I *was* on the docket for Wednesday, and I asked her, only half jokingly, "Do you know what I'm talking about?"

Ultimately, I *did* speak at the luncheon. And it was wonderful. It was only ten minutes (the other 50 minutes had to be filled with CLE credits, of course), but it was different from other speaking I had done. I wasn't a training session—it was an inspiration session. And I realized that *that* is what energized me. I challenged them to think differently about the practice of law generally, and how *they* wanted to practice law specifically.

This led to meetings about speaking to future groups, as well as my first coaching client—a lawyer.

God has *such* a sense of humor.

After I told my mentor about the PCWA speaking engagement, he said, "What do you think that means?" I confessed I had no idea. He laughed. I had, after the last problems with the CLE events, sworn off trying to do work connected with law in any way. And then God dropped this PCWA thing in my lap.

He (my mentor, not God) suggested that perhaps I was throwing out the whole bucket—or as my mom used to say, throwing out the baby with the bath water. As long as I was trying to get back into law in a traditional way, the door was going to slam. But maybe the real direction was to be that outside, objective voice that helped *other* attorneys change things from the inside.

My gifts were in challenging people to see things differently and helping them develop the plan and take the steps necessary to achieve their goals. My focus was to be on the relationships, not the training or the actual practicing of law. My law degree helped, because it gave me the language, the stories and the credibility to work with other attorneys in a way that non-lawyers would not be able to.

Which led me full circle, back to another belief I hold near and dear: all things work together for good. My decision to go to law school was probably not the right, or at least best, decision for me. But once I let go of the idea that it was wrong, or that I had to "do law" in a traditional way, I was able to see how it could "work together" with the gifts God *did* give me—for good.

And that makes it not such a bad decision after all.

CHAPTER 30

SMALL SOLUTIONS

On our tenth wedding anniversary, I worked with my husband's boss to get him some vacation time. I told her I was "kidnapping" him and wanted to leave on Friday for a drive down to Kansas City. She *loved* the idea and agreed to help me.

When I showed up at his office, he was on a ladder with his head stuck in the drop ceiling (probably running cables). She was at the base of the ladder, and when she saw me, she winked and, in her best "serious boss" voice, told him to come down off the ladder *right now*. He got real still for a minute, and we nearly burst out laughing. It was clear he was trying to figure out what he might have done while on a *ladder* to make her mad. And then when he saw *me*, his concern shifted from what he might have done to make *his boss* mad, to what he might have done to make his *wife* mad! It was quite amusing, actually.

Once we explained to him what was going on, he was definitely up for the adventure. So we headed out of town for a fun-filled weekend in Kansas City. Unfortunately, we had car trouble near the Iowa/Missouri border. We limped the car along to Bethany, where the dealership diagnosed a fuel pump issue, repaired it and sent us on our way, with several hundred dollars less to spend on "fun."

As it turned out, the fuel pump wasn't the problem.

It took us *nine hours* to make that three-hour drive, and by the time we got to Kansas City, it was too late to rent a car. Our tenth anniversary dinner was at an *Applebee's* because it was within walking distance of our hotel (nothing against Applebee's—just not where I had planned to have our celebratory dinner). The next day, my husband rented a car. And not just any car—a purple Hyundai. He said it would be easier to find. So now we have an ugly purple car *and* less money to spend on fun.

We called around, trying to find a place that could repair our car, but apparently every car in Kansas City needed repairs that weekend, and so it would be several weeks before they could get us in. Since we were only there for the weekend, that was a problem. We called Randy's older brother, Jeff, who had a mini-van. He agreed to rent a tow dolly and drive down on Sunday to pick up both our car and us.

When he showed up, we realized we needed some items to secure the car onto the dolly, so we eased it over to a nearby Home Depot. The "boys" discovered that the car, a green Dodge Neon with a spoiler for a front bumper, would not sit on the dolly. So in true "boys will be boys" fashion (the stereotypical mechanical version, not the sexual harassment version), they began plotting how they could build something to lift the car so the bumper would clear the part of the dolly at issue. I watched this for a bit and finally sighed impatiently, asking what I thought was an obvious question.

"Why don't you just take the bumper off?"

They looked at me, stunned, and then started laughing. Randy went into Home Depot, bought a set of Allen wrenches, and put a blanket on the black top under the car. Did I mention our anniversary was the end of July? And we were in Kansas City? The temperature (without the heat index) was over 100 degrees. We opened an umbrella to provide some shade, and Randy quickly removed the bumper, stashing it in the car. He then easily drove the car up onto the dolly for towing.

Problem solved.

The point of this story is not to point out the difficulties of our anniversary weekend (if I was going to do that, I would have started with our honeymoon, which included camping—in a tent—when the tornado sirens went off, horses passing gas on a narrow mountain pass and a speeding ticket). Instead, it's to point out that we often think that big problems need big, complicated solutions. That's rarely the case.

I've begun asking myself two questions. First, "What outcome do I want?" And second, "What's the easiest, best way to make that happen?"

With the car, the outcome I wanted was to get it on the tow dolly. The easiest way to make that happen was to take the bumper off. Was that the only way? No, of course not. But it was the *easiest*. It took the least amount of time *and* effort (and probably stress. I can only imagine what those two characters would have built to drag my car back to Des Moines).

This spring, I had the opportunity to speak to three business-writing classes at ISU. We spent a fair amount of time talking about resumes, and I suggested that one question they should always be asking is whether they were making it easy for the employer to hire them or easy to "file" their resume in the "round file." I reminded them that employers get many, *many* resumes for every position they post. As such, they are looking for quick ways to weed people out. Typos, profanity and weird color choices make it easy for employers to sort you out of contention right at the beginning. My boss at The University of Iowa once got a resume for a high-level position on green paper. The man's last name was Green, but guess where this attempt to "stand out" got his resume? And if you

Google "resume fails," you can entertain yourself for a good long time reading the less-than-brilliant things people do.

After the class, one ambitious young man asked if I would look at his resume. I appreciated his initiative, so I agreed. But when I received it, I just shook my head, wondering if he had heard anything I said in class. This was a resume he had obviously prepared well before the class, but I don't think it occurred to him to review it *after* my presentation. There were a number of problems with it, but overall, the impression it gave me was that he was disorganized, with little attention to detail. And he's studying to be an architect, where I would presume attention to detail is important if you want a house that will be standing for at least a few years.

The things I was talking to the class about were the easy things, and there are lots of tools to help people get it right. Things like spellcheck and grammar check; templates; and blog posts about how to write a great resume. If you can't be bothered to do the easy things, what will you do when faced with the hard things?

Of course, the easy things are sometimes the "grunt work." Checking your spelling is not nearly as much fun as the persuasive writing of the cover letter. Taking the bumper off the car is not as adventurous as building a ramp. But sometimes we simply don't take the time to think about *how* to make things easier.

Shortly after I began working with Curt, I told a friend that I had met someone more strategic than me. "No way," she said. So I told her the story of the gas pump. Curt took me with him to meet with an out-of-town client of his. Before we headed home, he filled up the car with fuel. Most people, if they try to "control" how much gas they put in, try to stop it at an even dollar amount. Not Curt. He stopped it at a point that had a penny at the end. When he got back in the car, I jokingly asked if he had "missed" (the even dollar amount). He said, "No—it's a strategy."

"A strategy?" I asked, clearly skeptical. He explained that when he got his credit card statement each month, he could easily determine which trips were business ones because they had that odd penny at the end. I'm sure my expression was priceless. Who *thinks* of that kind of stuff? Well, he does. It was brilliant, in part because of its simplicity. But you see, Curt had taken the time to think about the best way to quickly and easily determine whether something was a business or personal trip. It didn't require an app, an expensive software package, an accountant or anything other than simply ending on a penny when he bought gas. Easy. Effective. Efficient.

And my friend had to concede I might be right—I *had*, perhaps, met someone who was more strategic than me.

I hope he wasn't teasing me about that.

Lawyers, of course, are *not* known for keeping things simple, which was kind of a problem for me. But it's not usually because they are trying to increase their fees (although that may be true of some lawyers). Business lawyers are in the business of protecting their clients, but sometimes in their zealousness to protect their clients against every *possible* thing that *might* go wrong, they get in the way of good business getting done, or at least getting done easily. Which is why some people avoid lawyers.

When we lived in the tiny town of Hills, Iowa, our landlady was an elderly woman named Gladys. Gladys had the best rental agreement I've ever seen (that's not a legal opinion—just a personal one), but I suspect a lawyer had not reviewed it. It was just one paragraph long, noting the amount of rent and deposit, when rent was due and where it was to be paid. The rest of the paragraph essentially said that she agreed to do necessary repairs, and we agreed to leave the apartment in as good as, or better condition than when we found it. That was it. Can you guess how many problems we had with her? Zero.

The point of all of this is that simple is usually best. There is less confusion, less opportunity for problems and fewer misunderstandings. Although not everything can be as simple as a one-paragraph rental agreement or taking off a bumper, there's no reason to make things more complicated than they need to be. Let it go.

CHAPTER 31

VALUES

When I started law school, I had a scholarship. I could keep that scholarship for every year I was in the top one-third of my class. Unfortunately, my first year ranking did not permit me to receive the scholarship my second year. Law school is very competitive, and between that and having many other things on my plate (two very young children and a job, to name a few), my ranking slipped.

But that spring, I received great news—I had earned it back for my third year! However, one day shortly after the rankings came out, I was sitting out on the second-floor patio and heard other students discussing class rankings in conjunction with GPAs. It became apparent to me that a mistake had been made. My GPA was lower than those other students, yet my ranking was higher. That obviously could not be, and I became very concerned.

I needed that scholarship money, but it was clear to me that I had not actually qualified for it. It was an "ethical dilemma" turning point. But while some may have struggled with what to do, I did not. I went to the associate dean's office and explained to him what I had learned, finishing with, "Although I really need that money, I didn't apparently qualify for it."

He looked confused. How often do you think a law student showed up in the dean's office to turn down scholarship money? I'm not sure he quite knew what to do, so he simply said, "Well, if they've awarded it to you, it's yours." And at that point, I was fine with it. I had done what was necessary to act with integrity, and his decision about the money was made with that knowledge, so I could keep it.

Many people equate integrity with its dictionary definition—being honest and fair. And my law school example is just that. While it's true that some people would have said that it was the law school's mistake, and not my problem, taking advantage of a mistake feels dishonest to me. It's why I rarely play cutthroat cribbage! It doesn't feel like I've earned the win if it's dependent upon me catching and capitalizing on someone else's failure to see points. And it's one of the biggest problems I had with law. It was terrifying to make a mistake because your opposing counsel would take advantage of that, to the detriment of your *client*. But that's just not how I wanted to play the game. I'm not wired that way.

This showed up in a rather unusual way one year. One of the areas in which I practiced was employment law. I typically represented the plaintiffs—people who had (allegedly) been illegally discriminated against or sexually harassed, and who were bringing suit against their employer.

Most often, harassment cases included garden-variety behaviors, such as inappropriate statements and innuendos, leering and occasionally touching. The touching was usually putting an arm around a woman, touching the small of her back or unwelcome and inappropriate hugging. But one case went far beyond that—to a sexual assault.

As part of the process, discovery requests are sent to the opposing party. Discovery is simply a way to find out (i.e., "discover") what information the other party has. It includes three main written pieces (as well as depositions, which are not written, but oral):

interrogatories (written questions that must be answered under oath, in writing); requests for the production of documents (asking that certain documents be turned over); and requests for admission (asking the opposing party to admit certain things so you don't have to prove them at trial).

Requests for Admission typically cover very basic things: "Admit you're a resident of Iowa." "Admit Plaintiff was an employee of yours at the time in question." These are things you assume the other party isn't disputing, but that you don't want to waste time "proving" at trial.

However, I always made it a practice to also ask defendants to admit the ultimate question of fact; e.g., that the defendant had sexually harassed my client or illegally discriminated against my client. There was a strategic reason for this. The defendant would never admit it, of course, but on rare occasions, they might miss the deadline for returning those responses (30 days), which technically meant that they were deemed admitted. Which, in turn, theoretically meant that they would lose the case. And yes, I know that sounds like it goes against my aversion to taking advantage of mistakes, but it was so unlikely that opposing counsel would miss that particular deadline, I didn't give it much thought.

While deadlines for interrogatories and requests for production are rather "fluid," the deadline for requests for admission tends not to be. Attorneys rarely miss that deadline because of the severe consequences if they do. But oddly enough, that's exactly what happened in this case.

The lawyer for the defendant was an older attorney who had once been a judge, and so should have known better. I don't know why he missed it. But again, I am not a "cutthroat" player, and the discovery rules required that I reach out to him first, before filing any motions with the court. So I did. But he didn't respond to that. Nor any of the additional times I tried to contact him. So I finally filed a motion for summary judgment, because to *not* do so would have disadvantaged *my* client and put me at risk for malpractice.

But this is an unusual motion for a plaintiff to file, because this motion essentially says to the court, "The other side has no case, and you should dismiss it now, before we've spent a lot of time and money getting ready for trial." Plaintiffs are the ones who *file* cases, so it's rare that they want one dismissed.

But my motion essentially said that the defendant had not responded to the Requests for Admission. As such, they were deemed admitted, including the one that said, "Admit you sexually harassed Plaintiff." And because they had "admitted" the ultimate fact, my client was, by default, the "winner." So we weren't asking for it to be dismissed, per se, but rather that we be declared the winner. The only thing left for the court to decide then would be damages.

That's not quite how it played out, but that's a different war story for a different day (when I've had a strong drink). The point is, I only "took advantage" of his mistake when he left me no other options. Integrity meant that I wasn't pouncing on his mistake, but once it was clear he was not going to correct his mistake, despite knowing about it, I could pursue the motion with a clear conscience.

In my coaching practice, I start by asking people to identify their values. We explore what matters most to them, so that everything else we do lines up with their values. Curt does the same thing with his financial clients, reminding them (with memorable hand gestures) that values and actions have to line up. If they don't, one or the other must change.

But if you've ever read a book that talks about identifying your values, you will know there's a list of many, *many* values that you might choose from. Often, there is a winnowing process:

Pick the top 25, then out of those 25, choose the top 10, and then the top five. But what I found problematic was that there were some things that I believed to be universal values, such as family, faith, health and happiness. There are few people who don't value at least some of these. But if you choose those as your five, it becomes difficult to distinguish what makes *you* different.

So I implemented the *Wheel of Fortune* policy. It used to be that in the final round of this game show, the contestant was to choose five consonants and a vowel to try to solve the puzzle. But people began choosing the same letters (s, t, r, l, n, e) over and over, with only a few exceptions. So *Wheel* changed the rules and *gave* them those letters, and then had them choose a few more. The game was more interesting that way.

Likewise, I tell my clients that I will "give" them the universal values, and then ask them to choose five others. This helps me understand the *unique* drivers they possess so that we can better line up actions with values. If one of the "universal" drivers is of particular importance to someone, or if it plays out a bit differently for them, then I tell them to go ahead and list it.

And even though it's sometimes hard to hold onto those values, whether due to personal gain (like my scholarship money) or peer pressure, it's more miserable to *not* remain true.

Beauty is a value I hold, but I struggled to admit it. It sounded materialistic or shallow—surely there were other, more noble values to hold. But Bill Strickland, in his book *Making the Impossible Possible* has a different take on it, one that makes me say, "Yes! That's why it is important to me!"

In writing about his rather non-traditional inner city school and the beautiful things he has in it, he explains, "[The school] generates order and serenity and stability and optimism, things many of our students do not enjoy in abundance in their private lives. Poor people live in a world where beauty seems impossible.

We make it possible. Then the world and eventually the future look very different to them."

He goes on to report that, "[w]e put them in a beautiful place, give them a small taste of what a decent, dignified future might feel like, and that makes all the difference. The beauty we've designed into our center isn't window-dressing; it's an essential part of our success." And the success of his school and his students bears out this statement.

I once applied for a job at Legal Aid, mainly because it was part-time. At the time, I was the director of a non-profit in Urbandale, which was also a part-time gig, but I thought the Legal Aid job would pay better.

As I dropped my resume in the mail (pre-electronic submission), the only "word" I could think of was, "ugh." A few days later, I received a call inviting me in for an interview. My reaction was *not* "Yay! I'm so excited!" Instead it was, "Oh, for Pete's sake." My reactions were instinctively reminding me that a job at Legal Aid was *not* honoring my value of beauty, because Legal Aid is ugly most of the time.

Now, don't get me wrong—it's a great service, and I admire the attorneys who work there, but it's not right for *me*. Legal Aid clients often have difficulties that go far beyond legal ones. There may be economic struggles, educational deficiencies and often language barriers or other issues that make sorting out the legal ones even more difficult. All of those challenges would be overwhelming for me because I would want to help them with *everything*! Far beyond what I could actually *do*.

Like Strickland's students, my "spirit responds to and flourishes in an environment that provides [me] with order, purpose, opportunity and beauty." Beauty helps me see possibility, for myself *and* others. Beauty is the serenity of a lake, the energy of a great piece of music and the joy of a child's laughter. These things I value; they nurture my soul and make me a better person. But if I had ignored this value and tried to work at Legal Aid (which sounds like a more *noble* value), I would have been miserable. I would have been exhausted, drained and difficult to live with. I know that about myself.

I have had to learn how to hold on tightly to my values. Despite knowing that when I try to live out my life based on what *other* people value it never ends well, living my own values can still be challenging. When people unfriend me or even verbally attack me because of my political beliefs, it's hard to hold fast.

When it's easier to distance myself from those who are different rather than show kindness, it's hard to act consistently with the value of kindness. And when I really need that scholarship money, it's hard to live that integrity value.

But trust me on this—you will regret it if you don't follow your values.

⊷ ⊶

Patrick Lencioni, in his book *The Advantage,* talks about core values of an organization and tells a great story about Southwest Airlines. Southwest, as many of you know, has humor as a value. This comes across even in traditionally *non*humorous situations, like the safety "talk" that the flight attendants give at the beginning of each flight. Southwest has raised this mind-numbing public service announcement to an art. There are YouTube videos of flight attendants rapping about safety.

Although most passengers appreciate this, not everyone does. There was a woman who sent a letter stating that safety was a serious topic and shouldn't be joked about. Southwest could have caved, sent her an apologetic letter and advised its flight attendants to be more serious about safety, but they didn't, because that would have gone against their core value of humor. Instead, they sent her an epic letter consisting of just three words: "We'll miss you."

People pleasers like me would have a hard time sending that letter. But it speaks to the absolute clarity Southwest has about its values, understanding that they might not be for everyone. They are so committed to their values that they are willing to suffer for them (in the form of lost customers). But that's one of the ways you can identify your core values. What is so vital, so integral to who you are that you are willing to suffer for it rather than give it up?

For me, integrity is so critical that I was willing to give up scholarship money that I desperately needed. I was willing to apologize to my former boss because I was wrong, despite the tremendous resistance I had to him. Beauty is so important to me that my instincts tried to warn me about the Legal Aid job with *verbal* responses to both applying and getting an interview.

Knowing what your values are is critical to making the right decisions in your life; you can't make good decisions based on other people's values. Hold on to those values, and let go of what other people think you should do. Although they undoubtedly have your best interests at heart, their decisions are based on *their* values, not yours.

CHAPTER 32

FORGIVENESS

On Easter weekend, there is a prayer vigil at Plymouth Church. It runs from the end of the Good Friday service through the start of the Sunrise Service on Easter morning. It's that in-between time between the horror and the sorrow of Good Friday and the joy and euphoria of Easter—a time of waiting, and of watching.

Procedurally, there is a sign-up sheet, divided into half-hour increments. You sign up for a slot, show up and sit quietly in prayer during your thirty-minute time frame. You are welcome to sign up with a friend or prayer partner as well. There is a book for people to sign their names and the time they were there and offer comments, and there are books on a small round table to offer guidance, should you need or desire that.

There are chairs, big, comfortable pillows, and sometimes prayer shawls for your comfort. It's a small, cozy space at the foot of the Christ candle, and I always look forward to that time alone with God. Truly, it is one of my favorite days of the year.

This is due, in part, to the fact that most of the time the prayer chapel at Plymouth is *not* particularly quiet. Whoever designed the space apparently didn't put much thought into its location. It sits between two bathrooms, across from the coffee shop and just around the corner from Waveland Hall, which is always a busy place. It's near the stairs that go to the offices, and if you come in the west door on the circle drive, you often go past the chapel to get to the sanctuary or the elevators that take you upstairs to the Sunday School classrooms, the youth room and the rehearsal halls. And to top it off, the pop machine is just down the hall.

In other words—it's rarely quiet in the prayer chapel.

But on this one day, there are signs on the restrooms asking people to use a different one. The coffee shop is closed, and other than the Saturday night service, Waveland Hall is used only for those quietly walking the labyrinth. There are signs reminding people of the prayer vigil and asking them to walk quietly through the halls.

This year, when I signed up for the 9 a.m. time slot, I noticed that my friend Rita had signed up for 8:30. A fellow accompanist (who plays for the Kinder Choir and the first-grade Cherubs) signed up for 9:30. She is very conscientious, so I knew she would be prompt.

When I arrived at church, I was about 10 minutes early. Not wanting to disrupt my friend's time, I went instead to the labyrinth in Waveland Hall for contemplative walking and praying. I decided that this would be a good way to get in the right frame of mind for my prayer time in the chapel, so I stepped onto the labyrinth and began to slowly walk the path. My breathing quieted, and my steps became deliberate.

I began to compare the labyrinth to life—you know where you want to end up, but getting there is often full of twists and turns, and you can't always see where you're going next. If I tried to see the whole path before starting, it would take me a long time to even *start*, let alone arrive. And in the case of walking the labyrinth, I might end up spending the full ten minutes looking at it, trying to figure out where it went, rather than just starting, putting one foot in front of the other and taking the turns as they came.

By the time it was my turn in the prayer chapel, I felt calm and relaxed, ready to sit quietly for my 30 minutes. Unfortunately, that turned out to be the calm before the (emotional) storm. When I went in, I was surprised to see someone I didn't know in the chapel instead of Rita. I began to worry that I had shown up at the wrong time. I frantically tried to remember, without popping up to go out and check the schedule. No, I concluded. I knew I was there at the right time. Well, then, maybe my friend had switched her time. But this woman did not get up and leave, which she should have done had she been in the 8:30 slot. I began to get more and more agitated. What was going on? Why was she taking up *my* time slot?

I tried to calm myself down. I acknowledged the irony of being angry with someone *while I was supposed to be praying.* I told myself it didn't matter if she was in there—I should just focus on what I was there for. I tried praying *for* her. None of it worked. I could not let go of my resentment.

At 9:20, she wrote in the book and *finally* left. I jumped up to see who it was and what time she was to be there. I didn't recognize the name, but I did note that she was there from 8:30 to 9:20. And she wrote that she was "refreshed" after her time in the chapel. I, of course, responded by being incensed. She was *refreshed?* Well I'm glad *one* of us was, because she had *ruined* my time there! Didn't she know the "rules?" Why couldn't people do the right thing?! And now I had only 10 minutes, I was in a decidedly *un*prayerful mood, and I was angry with myself for being so petty.

As I stepped out of the chapel promptly at the conclusion of my time (I certainly wasn't going to be like *that woman* who stole *my* time!), I looked at the sign-up sheet. Rita was still on the schedule at 8:30. But this other woman was also signed up for that slot. What had happened?

I called Rita and asked her about it. She gave a short laugh and said, "Funny you should ask." She told me that she noticed this other woman signed up in her slot. When she asked her about it, she discovered that the woman had called the office to ask if more than one person could sign up for the same slot.

Misunderstanding her question, the office person said that yes, people could sign up to do it together. What she missed was the meaning of "together." There weren't multiple *openings* in the same time slot, but rather the option to sign up *with someone you knew.* This woman didn't know Rita and didn't ask her if it was okay to share her time slot. And Rita didn't want to "correct" her, so she simply didn't show up—she let this other woman have her time. And then, because the woman believed it was okay to be there "with" someone else, she didn't feel the need to leave at 9:00, when it was my turn.

Now I was really upset. My friend had been "cheated" out of her time slot, and I had lost most of mine. It wasn't *fair.* Why couldn't people do the right thing? Why couldn't they do what they said they would do? What was *wrong* with people?!

Part of the problem was that I was coming off a week where others had not done what they said they would do. I was supposed to learn whether I had been chosen for a part-time job, but the employer didn't call as promised. My husband had failed to do what he said *he* would on several things. And now this. It felt like *no one* was doing what they said they would do.

That was complicated by who I am. A few years ago, I did a beta test for a new assessment Marcus Buckingham was introducing, called *StandOut.* Building on his success working with strengths-based leadership, this assessment was designed to tell you what your greatest contributions to the *team* were. My two? Equalizer and Advisor. What that meant was that I "combine doing what is best with doing what is right." Practically speaking, that means that my kryptonite is people who do *not* do what is right or best. It twists me up in knots and then yanks—hard. It makes me slow to forgive—myself as well as others.

What all this has to do with the prayer vigil "incident" is that, despite *knowing* that I was being petty and ridiculous, I couldn't let go of my resentment. It was rude, it was inconsiderate, and it was uncalled for. Originally, I thought I was describing her behavior with that last sentence. But as I reread it, I realize it applied equally to my own.

Of course, how she had behaved was *my* perspective. Her perspective was likely that she had called the office to see if more than one person could be in the prayer chapel at the same time, and was told that yes, that was fine. If either Rita or I had taken the time to correct the misunderstanding, the whole situation could have been avoided. She was probably not *intentionally* interfering with our time.

I hate it when I get stuck in anger or make it all about me, especially when I recognize that I am being unreasonable. So today I started thinking about *how* to let go. Awareness is not enough—I was well aware of the fact that I was being ridiculous, yet I could not seem to let it go. Berating myself doesn't work—I just felt worse, because I was "failing" at being kind and generous. And expecting others to behave in conformity with what *I* believe to be "right or best" *clearly* doesn't work.

Curt has always told me to focus on what's important and ignore the rest. That can mean a variety of things, depending on context (kind of an equal opportunity piece of advice), but in this situation, it meant I should have either spoken up (kindly) or let it go. Instead, I allowed her to distract me, aggravate me and steal my time and my peace of mind.

When I first began talking to my editor about the book, I said, "You know, there's a lot in here about *what* or *who* I need(ed) to let go of, and *when* I should have let it go (as opposed to when I *did* let it go), and even *why* I needed to let go. But not much about *how*. Do you think that's important?"

She acknowledged that it was a good question but didn't provide an answer right then, preferring instead to see how the book would develop. I'm not sure even now that I have a good answer to "how." But then, as I looked at my "list" of chapters and topics, I began to analyze them more closely. I first divided them into things that were easy to let go of, and those that were hard.

Some were hard because I felt I had no control over the situation, like the death of my dad. Others were difficult because of the shame associated with letting the thing go, like my house. Still others were hard because of fear—fear of making a mistake or the uncertainty of what would happen if I let go. Some things were hard simply because they were a habit. But I realized that each of these required a different "how" of letting go.

I don't know that I have any advice on this point. Yes, being aware helps. Yes, looking at pros and cons *within the context of what you are trying to achieve* helps. Yes, focusing on what is important and ignoring (or at least minimizing) the rest helps. But "helps" is different from "does." Letting go, or even simply opening up is still a struggle for me. It is my prayer that this book will help someone who might also be struggling with letting go, or opening up to new possibilities, perspectives and opportunities.

Writing this book and revising it has been, at times, extraordinarily difficult. I've cried tears of sorrow *and* shame. I've awakened in the night asking, "Can I *really* publish this book?" I've worried that the things I've written might hurt others, and I've rewritten or even pulled chapters when I'm convinced the answer is yes. I've even told my editor, only half-jokingly, that I may not be able to show my face in public after it's published; I may need to move.

Ultimately, though, I hope people will look at this book in the same way that Mike Rowe, the incredibly smart and down-to-earth star of *Dirty Jobs,* thinks of a friend and former employee of his. In writing about this brave woman and her appearance in a documentary, he wrote, "But mostly, [the movie] made me very proud of my friend, and others like her. It's a hell of a thing to realize everything you believe is not what you thought it was. And *it's even harder to confess your mistakes to the world and start over.*" (Emphasis mine).

It *has* been hard to face up to the things—and the people—that were not as I believed them to be. And to confess my flaws and mistakes to the world and start over? Oh, yes —brutal. But it is also freeing.

This is me.

I love the saying, "Don't judge me by my past. I don't live there anymore." And this is the true joy of the Easter message—we don't have to live in those past mistakes any longer. We are forgiven. We get a brand new second chance (or third, fourth or fifth). Yes, I've had difficult times—we *all* have. But I am stronger because of the things I've been through. I'm still standing. And I'm going to move forward by being courageous. I'm going to hold things loosely, allowing those things to stay that are meant to stay, and letting go—gently—of those things that are meant to leave.

After I wrote this and sent it off to my editor, I decided it was unfinished—not the chapter so much as the event. I had been writing in a *Starbucks* (I had already *been* to *Grounds for Celebration*, which is my preferred coffee shop), and it was still early in the afternoon, so I hopped in my car and headed back to church—to the prayer chapel, which was predictably noisy.

I had forgotten that, in addition to all the things I had listed above, the preschool *playground* is on the other side of the beautiful stained glass. The kids were joyfully shouting and playing in the warm sunshine, sheltered from the wind. And there were elderly, hard-of-hearing men wandering the hall with all the church history photos, talking about what a great minister David Ruhe had been (he retired in December). Although it wasn't quiet, both the children and the elderly—the bookends of life—made me smile. As the older gentleman continued to show his friend around, he pointed out the prayer chapel. The other man confessed to feeling a little lost in our big church.

And that seemed like the perfect metaphor. I wasn't physically lost in the church, of course, but I had been spiritually lost in the prayer chapel on Saturday. I had let resentment get in the way of my quiet prayer time. I didn't try to fix the problem that day, choosing instead to sit and stew about her "rudeness." But on *this* day, the day after Easter, I quietly prayed for forgiveness and sat in stillness until it came. I was so glad I came back for that "lesson" of being lost, found and forgiven.

And that is the real blessing of letting go and remaining open to possibilities. We cannot ask for forgiveness—whether from God, others, or even ourselves—until we let go of the negative emotions. We can't experience new opportunities while we're holding on tightly to what's comfortable.

Great things cannot come into our life until we are willing to let go of bad, and even the merely good. *How* we do that will depend on the situation and why we're hanging on. It is not always easy, and sometimes it's painful. But the more loosely we hold things in the first place, the easier and less painful it is for things to naturally flow in and out of our lives.

It is my hope for you that somewhere in this book you will have seen yourself. And perhaps in seeing yourself, you can choose to let go of whatever it is that is holding you back, and instead, open up to new perspectives, opportunities, and people. Let go of the past and its hurts, embrace the future and its possibilities, and live well, right where you are now.

~Jean